Tony Turnbull

THE ONLY RECIPES YOU'LL EVER NEED

4 WAYS TO COOK ALMOST EVERYTHING

Photographs by Romas Foord

Quadrille
PUBLISHING

HOW TO USE THIS BOOK

We're terrible creatures of habit, aren't we? We think we're free spirits, constantly seeking out the new, yet when it comes to it, we go back to the same old, same old. Especially with what we cook. We see a packet of mince in the fridge, we make spaghetti bolognese; we see a box of eggs, we make a cheese omelette; we see a tin of sweetcorn, we make… Actually, no one ever knows what to do with a tin of sweetcorn.

We may even make these things pretty well, but it does get boring. No matter how exotic the food programmes we love to watch, or however much chefs exhort us to take inspiration from what looks freshest at the market, we are stuck in the same old rut.

It doesn't help that when you open the fridge door you are confronted by the same array of ingredients. If you are like me, you probably do the weekly shop on autopilot, putting the same things in your trolley. Or even more habit forming, you do your grocery shopping online. None of that exactly encourages you to try something new.

So what I want to do here is help you ring the changes. Not by ditching all the things you know and love, but by showing you that with a few simple changes, a small twist here or there, you can look at an ingredient afresh and take your cooking in a different direction. Fancy a risotto? You'll find four variations on the theme. Chicken thighs for dinner? There are four suggestions for how to serve those too. In fact you'll find four things to do with all the most common dishes and ingredients, from soups and salads to pies and noodles. With over 270 recipes included, you could sit down to something different every week day for a year. (Not that I'm advocating that – I want to help you branch out, not make you a culinary commitment phobe.)

OK, there's a trick at work here. When I first came to create my column of The Only Four Recipes You'll Ever Need for *The Times* newspaper, it immediately became clear that if I was to fit four recipes plus photos onto just two pages, something would have to give.

First off, it meant I couldn't include long lists of ingredients or any complicated processes. The dishes had to be straightforward, with a maximum of three, maybe four steps. No loss there because I think that's the way most of us like to cook anyway. Sure, we might go the extra mile when friends are coming round at the weekend, but for everyday – the kind of cooking this book is mainly aimed at – the quicker and simpler the better.

Second, I've had to be economical with the language. If it reads a little brusquely, as if you are being instructed by a sergeant major with English as a second language, I apologise, especially to my old English teacher, who'll be appalled by my liberties with grammar. But mainly I've got there by omitting all the waffle most cookbooks are full of, all those instructions to beat the eggs *'in a large bowl with a whisk'* or to cook the stew *'in a casserole dish large enough to contain all the meat, vegetables and stock'*. Some things are too obvious to spell out, but for what's it worth, I include 10 tips opposite that will make you a better cook whoever's recipes you are following.

We are all so overloaded with information these days, but somehow it never seems to make our choices any easier. That's why I've adopted a 'less is more' approach with this book. Think of it as a capsule wardrobe for the kitchen: simple recipes, short shopping lists and concise instructions – I really hope it will be the only cookbook you'll ever need.

TOP 10 TIPS

SEASON CONFIDENTLY

Amateur cooks are too timid, professionals sometimes too heavy handed, but judicious seasoning is the single easiest way to improve your cooking. Generally add salt and pepper early in the cooking process to unlock the flavours and you'll find you don't need to season at the table, meaning less salt in the long run.

DON'T BE SCARED OF HEAT

Again, something that marks inexperienced cooks from professionals. Heat is good. Be bold. Get your pans properly hot, especially when searing a steak or using a wok. Accept that there will be smoke, turn on the extractor fan, and get on with it. For the same reason, always preheat the oven. Yes, it really does make a difference.

SEAR IN FLAVOUR

Colour is flavour, and achieving a Marmitey golden brown crust on your rib of beef or fried mushrooms will improve the final result no end. The trick is to ensure your ingredient is absolutely dry (blot it on kitchen paper if necessary) and well seasoned before adding to a hot pan. Don't stir or turn it until the bottom is browned, and never crowd the pan as this will lower the temperature and it won't brown. Once it's caramelised, you can obviously turn the heat down to cook it through without burning.

GET YOUR OIL HOT

Always heat the pan and oil before adding your ingredients. You want to be able to hear a sizzling noise when they go in. If you can't, nothing is hot enough, and you run the risk of boiling your food when you meant to fry it. And then it will be wan and tasteless (see searing above).

BUT DON'T BROWN THE GARLIC

Or the onions. Or the leeks. Vegetables like these often need to be fried in butter or oil to bring out their natural sweetness before adding other ingredients, and they need a gentler hand. Cook over a medium heat and stir regularly until soft and translucent, anything up to 10 minutes. A little colour isn't the end of the world, but burn them and you have to start again.

CHOP EVENLY

People get very excited about knife skills, thinking the most important thing is to build up their speed. It's not. Take as long as you like, but DO cut things into uniform sizes so that they cook evenly. And remember, cut thinner for fast cooking (e.g. stir-fries) and thicker for slow cooking (e.g. casseroles).

SIMMERING ISN'T THE SAME AS BOILING

OK, they're related, but simmering, a gentle bubbling of the liquid, is for cooking, e.g. poaching chicken; full-on boiling is for driving off liquid, e.g. reducing a stock to concentrate the flavour. Choose accordingly. Cook potatoes at a galloping boil, for example, and they are more likely to collapse and become waterlogged. Not nice.

KEEP TASTING

If *Masterchef* has taught you one thing, it's that you should taste your food as you go along. I don't know how sweet you like your rice pudding or how spicy you like your stir-fries, but if you stick a finger or spoon in occasionally, you can decide for yourself. All things are adjustable, and much easier as you go along.

DON'T BE A SLAVE TO THE DETAIL

Only baking requires accurate measurements, everything else you can pretty much make up according to taste. The recipes in this book all serve four, so remember you'll be eating a quarter of everything you put in. I find that helps to focus the mind when deciding how much chilli, cream or butter you want to add.

DON'T FRET ABOUT TIMING

When people say they have a problem with timing, they mean with getting everything to finish cooking at the same time. But that's not what timing is; timing is about making sure it DOESN'T all come together at the same time. Space it out so you have time to cope. Vegetables will hold in a warm oven, meat is always better for resting, and frankly things taste better when only lukewarm. Except fish. I hate lukewarm fish.

Editorial Director Anne Furniss

Creative Director Helen Lewis

Editor Louise McKeever

Designer Gemma Hogan

Photographer Romas Foord

Production Director Vincent Smith

Production Controller Leonie Kellman

First published in 2013 by
Quadrille Publishing Ltd
Alhambra House
27–31 Charing Cross Road
London WC2H 0LS
www.quadrille.co.uk

British Library Cataloguing-in-Publication Data
A catalogue record for this book is available from the British Library.

ISBN: 978 184949 286 7
Printed in China

NOTE: All recipes in this book serve four.

LIGHT DISHES

MAIN DISHES

DESSERTS

DRINKS

LIGHT
DISHES

BUTTERNUT SQUASH AND GINGER

1 large butternut squash, peeled
5cm knob of ginger
A large knob of butter
250ml white wine
1l chicken or vegetable stock
Single cream and black pepper, to serve

1 Roughly dice the butternut squash and chop the ginger. Place both into a saucepan with the butter. Cover and sweat over a gentle heat for about 30 minutes, stirring occasionally, or until the squash is soft.

2 Add the wine and cook uncovered until it has evaporated. Add the stock and bring up to a simmer. Purée using a stick blender. Serve with a swirl of cream and a sprinkling of black pepper.

MINESTRONE

4 tbsp olive oil
1 small onion, diced
2 carrots, diced
2 leeks, diced
2 garlic cloves, chopped
1¼l chicken or vegetable stock
2 small tomatoes, chopped
125g small pasta shapes
Freshly grated Parmesan, to serve

1 Heat the oil in a pan and cook the onion, carrots, leeks and garlic over a low heat, until soft but not coloured, about 10 minutes.

2 Season and add the stock and the tomatoes. Bring to a simmer, add the pasta and cook for about 10 minutes or until the pasta is al dente. Serve with a sprinkling of Parmesan.

ROAST TOMATO

1kg ripe tomatoes
A large handful of basil, shredded
4 garlic cloves, unpeeled
2 tbsp olive oil
600ml hot chicken or vegetable stock

1 Cut the tomatoes in half and place cut side up in a roasting tray. Scatter over the basil and garlic cloves, drizzle with the oil and season well. Roast at 180°C/Gas mark 4 for an hour or until the tomatoes are soft and the edges are charred. Let cool slightly.

2 Squeeze the garlic out of their skin and place in a blender with the tomatoes and their juices. Blend, adding enough stock until a thick soup consistency. Season and serve.

VEGETABLE

1¼l vegetable stock
1 small leek, diced
1 celery stick, diced
100g broad beans
100g peas
50g green beans or asparagus, roughly sliced
A handful of chopped parsley

1 Bring the stock to the boil. Add the leek and celery and simmer for 10 minutes or until the vegetables are soft. Season.

2 Add the broad beans, peas and green beans or asparagus and simmer for a further 10 minutes, adding the parsley for the last 2 minutes. Serve.

CLASSIC SOUPS

SPINACH AND HAM

200g spinach
Butter, for greasing
4 slices of ham, torn into pieces
4 eggs
2 tbsp double cream
A handful of freshly grated Parmesan

1 Cook the spinach in a microwave or a dry pan until wilted. Let cool then squeeze out as much water as you can.

2 Butter 4 small ramekins. Divide the spinach and ham between them. Crack an egg into each and season well. Top each with a little cream and some Parmesan.

3 Place the ramekins in a roasting tin half filled with boiling water. Bake in the oven for 12 minutes at 190°C/Gas mark 5. Serve.

BAKED EGGS

SMOKED HADDOCK

150–200ml double cream
100–120g smoked haddock
Butter, for greasing
4 eggs
1 tbsp roughly chopped dill

1 Put the cream in a saucepan with the haddock. Bring to the boil, cover and simmer for 2 minutes. Remove the haddock and leave to cool.

2 Butter 4 small ramekins, season, then crack in the eggs. Place the ramekins in a roasting tin half filled with boiling water. Bake in the oven at 180°C/Gas mark 4 for 10–12 minutes.

3 Meanwhile, bring the cream back to a simmer, skin and flake the haddock into the cream with the dill. Season. Simmer until the sauce thickens and serve over the eggs.

MUSHROOM AND TARRAGON

1 small onion, finely chopped
150g button mushrooms, finely chopped
A knob of butter, extra for greasing
A few sprigs of tarragon
4 eggs
4 tsp double cream
A handful of grated Gruyére

1 Fry the onion and mushrooms in the butter for 6–8 minutes until soft. Add the tarragon and take off the heat.

2 Butter 4 small ramekins and divide the mushroom mixture between them. Crack in an egg, season, and top with some cream and a sprinkling of Gruyére.

3 Place the ramekins into a roasting tin half filled with boiling water. Oven bake for 10–12 minutes at 190°C/Gas mark 5. Serve.

CUMIN, FENNEL AND CHILLI

½ tsp cumin seeds; 2 tsp fennel seeds;
1 red onion, finely chopped; A pinch of chilli flakes;
400g tin of chopped tomatoes; 1 tsp grated ginger;
Butter, for greasing; 4 eggs

1 Toast the cumin and fennel seeds in a dry frying pan for 1 minute. Add a little oil with the onion and chilli. Cook, stirring occasionally, until softened. Add the tomatoes and the ginger. Cook gently, for about 10 minutes, until thickened.

2 Butter 4 small ramekins. Half fill with the tomato mixture. Crack an egg on top. Season well.

3 Place the ramekins in a roasting tin half filled with boiling water. Oven bake for 10–12 minutes at 190°C/Gas mark 5. Serve.

CHICKEN AND PESTO

125g plain flour; 2 eggs; 250ml milk;
50g butter, melted, extra for frying; 2 shallots, sliced;
1 garlic clove, crushed; 350g cooked chicken;
200ml crème fraîche; 150g fresh pesto;
A handful of breadcrumbs; 150g Gruyére, grated

1 Mix the flour, eggs and a pinch of salt. Gradually whisk in enough milk for a silky batter and add the butter. Add a spoonful to a hot, oiled pan. Cook for 1 minute, flip and cook for 30 seconds. Repeat. Keep warm.

2 Fry the shallots and garlic in butter for 5 minutes or until soft. Add the chicken and créme fraîche, cook until thickened. Stir in the pesto. Divide between the pancakes and roll up.

3 Place in an ovenproof dish, sprinkle with breadcrumbs and cheese. Grill for 3 minutes until bubbling and golden. Serve.

LEEK AND MUSHROOM

125g plain flour; 2 eggs; 250ml milk;
50g butter, melted, extra for frying; 2 leeks, sliced;
2 handfuls of mushrooms, sliced;
1 garlic clove, crushed; 250ml double cream;
350g cooked chicken; A handful of chopped tarragon

1 Make the pancakes following step 1 for the Chicken and Pesto recipe. Keep warm.

2 Fry the leeks, mushrooms and garlic in a little butter over a medium heat until browned. Season. Add the cream and cook until thickened. Stir in the chicken. Add the tarragon and divide between the pancakes. Roll up. Serve.

SWEETCORN

150g plain flour
1 tsp baking powder
150ml milk
50g butter, melted
198g tin of sweetcorn
1 green chilli, finely chopped
½ green pepper, finely chopped
Grilled bacon and tomatoes, to serve

1 Mix together the flour, baking powder, milk and butter to make a smooth batter. Add the drained sweetcorn, chilli and pepper.

2 Heat a splash of oil in a pan. Add the sweetcorn batter in batches, and cook for about 90 seconds on each side. Serve with some bacon and grilled tomatoes.

SPINACH AND RICOTTA

125g plain flour
2 eggs
250ml milk
50g butter, melted
200g spinach
4 tbsp ricotta
A handful of freshly grated Parmesan
Freshly grated nutmeg

1 Make the pancakes following step 1 for the Chicken and Pesto recipe. Keep warm.

2 Meanwhile, cook the spinach for 2 minutes in the microwave, transfer to a sieve and squeeze out the water. Roughly chop and stir through the ricotta, Parmesan and nutmeg. Season. Place a spoonful of the mixture onto each pancake. Roll up. Serve.

SAVOURY PANCAKES

HAM, NECTARINE AND MOZZARELLA

2 nectarines
8 slices of Parma ham, roughly torn
1 large ball of mozzarella, roughly torn
1 red chilli, finely chopped
A small handful of mint, chopped
Zest and juice of 1 lemon

1 Stone and slice the nectarines. Arrange the slices on a serving platter with the ham and mozzarella. Scatter over the chilli, mint and lemon zest.

2 Dress with the lemon juice and olive oil. Season. Serve.

PANZANELLA

4 slices of sourdough
6 tbsp olive oil
6 ripe tomatoes, lightly crushed
1 cucumber, peeled and diced
4 shallots, thinly sliced
2 garlic cloves, finely chopped
2 tbsp red wine vinegar
A handful of basil leaves, torn
1 little gem lettuce, torn

1 Brush the slices of sourdough with oil, sprinkle with a little salt and bake for 10 minutes at 180°C/Gas mark 4. Break into bite-sized pieces.

2 Combine the tomatoes and cucumber in a large bowl with all the remaining ingredients. Mix well. Season. Serve.

CAESAR

2 small garlic cloves; 30g freshly grated Parmesan;
1 tbsp Dijon mustard; Juice of 1 lemon;
5 anchovy fillets, extra for serving;
200ml olive oil, extra for frying; 2 cos lettuces, torn;
1 small ciabatta loaf, crusts removed;
2 boiled eggs; Cooked chicken (optional)

1 Place the garlic, Parmesan, mustard, lemon juice and anchovies into a food processor. Mix well and, with the motor still running, add the oil in a slow trickle.

2 Place the lettuce into a serving bowl. Cut the bread into small cubes and fry in oil until crispy, then drain on kitchen paper.

3 Pour the dressing over the leaves, add the croûtons and serve with extra anchovies, halved boiled eggs and some cooked chicken if you like.

GREEK WATERMELON

8 tomatoes, roughly chopped
1 small cucumber, roughly chopped
A handful of pitted black olives
2 slices of watermelon, flesh cut into chunks
A small handful of mint, roughly chopped
120g feta
4 tbsp olive oil
2 tbsp red wine vinegar

1 Combine the tomatoes, cucumber, olives and watermelon in a serving bowl. Add the mint and crumble over the feta.

2 Dress with some olive oil and vinegar. Season, toss and serve.

ASIAN

2 tbsp honey
A small knob of ginger, grated
4 tbsp soy sauce
2 tbsp rice vinegar
2 tbsp sesame oil
75ml vegetable oil

1 Warm the honey in a small pan over a low heat to make it liquid. Squeeze the ginger over a bowl to collect the juice. Add the soy, vinegar and warm honey and combine. Add both oils and whisk to form a warm dressing. Serve with a chicken or seafood salad.

CLASSIC

50ml white wine vinegar
200ml olive oil
1 tsp Dijon mustard
A pinch of fine sugar
A pinch of salt

1 Whisk together all the ingredients. Serve drizzled over your salad.

HERBY

5 tbsp olive oil
2 tbsp lemon juice
A handful of parsley, finely chopped
A handful of mint leaves, finely chopped
1 tbsp finely chopped chives

1 Whisk together all the ingredients. Serve drizzled over your salad.

CREAMY

2 tbsp white wine vinegar
5 tbsp olive oil
1 tsp wholegrain mustard
2 tbsp crème fraîche
A pinch of salt
A pinch of pepper
A handful of parsley, chopped

1 Whisk together all the ingredients. Serve drizzled over your salad.

SALAD DRESSINGS

AUBERGINE

2–3 aubergines; 2 garlic cloves, crushed;
2 tbsp tahini; Juice of 1 lemon;
A pinch of ground cumin; 100g natural yoghurt;
1 tbsp olive oil; ½ a pomegranate; Toasted flatbread

1 Prick the aubergines a few times with a fork and, using a skewer, hold over a gas flame. Cook for 10 minutes or until charred all over. Alternatively, use a barbecue or, failing that, oven cook for 40 minutes at 200°C/Gas mark 6.

2 Once the aubergine is charred and has collapsed, cool, scrape out the flesh and place in a colander to drain any excess liquid.

3 Mash the flesh with a fork, add garlic, tahini, lemon juice, cumin and yoghurt. Season. Drizzle with oil and scatter with pomegranate seeds. Serve with the flatbread.

BEETROOT AND MINT

200g beetroot
2 tbsp horseradish sauce
75ml natural yoghurt
Half a handful of mint, chopped
Toasted flatbread

1 Sprinkle the beetroot with salt, wrap in foil and bake at 180°C/Gas mark 4 for 1 hour or until tender. Cool, then peel.

2 Using a hand blender, purée the beetroot with the horseradish and the yoghurt. Sprinkle over the mint. Season. Serve with the flatbread.

DIPS

CANNELLINI BEAN

2 garlic cloves
2 anchovy fillets
1 small chilli, deseeded
1 tsp chopped rosemary
400g tin of cannellini beans
Juice of 1 lemon
2 tbsp olive oil
Toasted sourdough

1 Crush the garlic, anchovies, chilli and rosemary using a pestle and mortar. Add the beans and roughly squash to form a chunky purée.

2 Add the lemon juice, olive oil and some black pepper. Combine. Serve with the toasted sourdough.

CHICKPEA

410g tin of chickpeas
3 garlic cloves
Juice of 1 lemon
1 tbsp tahini
2 tbsp olive oil
Handful of toasted pine nuts
Half a bunch of parsley, roughly chopped
Toasted flatbread

1 Rinse the chickpeas, reserving a little of the liquid. Place the chickpeas in a blender with the garlic, lemon juice and tahini. Season (adding plenty of salt). Pulse until smooth, adding the reserved liquid as needed to reach a smooth consistency.

2 Put the houmous into a bowl, drizzle with the olive oil and scatter over pine nuts and parsley. Serve with the flatbread.

SMOKED MACKEREL

MACKEREL AND BACON SALAD

500g salad potatoes; 6 rashers of smoked bacon;
A handful of broad beans; 6 tbsp olive oil;
2 tbsp red wine vinegar; 1 tsp English mustard;
1 small red onion; 4 smoked mackerel fillets

1 Boil the potatoes in salted water for about 10 minutes or until tender. Grill the bacon until crispy and cut into pieces. Boil the broad beans in salted water for about 5 minutes or until tender.

2 Whisk together the oil, vinegar and mustard. Slice the red onion very thinly and shred the mackerel and place in a salad bowl. Cut the warm potatoes into halves or quarters and add to the onions and mackerel, along with the beans and bacon. Dress with the vinaigrette. Season. Serve.

MACKEREL GRATIN

100g butter, extra for greasing; 2 large onions, sliced;
4 large potatoes; 4 smoked mackerel fillets, shredded;
400ml double cream; 70g watercress

1 Melt 90g of the butter in a large pan and add the onions. Cover and cook gently until very soft, about 30 minutes. Stir regularly. Meanwhile, peel the potatoes and slice very thinly, ideally using a mandoline.

2 Butter a baking dish and cover the bottom with half of the sliced potatoes. Season and add half of the onions. Spread the mackerel over the onions. Add the rest of the onions and top with the remaining potatoes.

3 Pour over the cream, dot with the rest of the butter and cook at 180°C/Gas mark 4 for about an hour or until the potatoes are soft and golden. Serve with watercress.

MACKEREL PÂTÉ

4 smoked mackerel fillets
A knob of butter
4 tsp crème fraîche
4 tsp creamed horseradish
A small handful of parsley
Zest and juice of 1 lemon
Toasted slices of bread
Lemon wedges, to serve

1 Place the fillets, butter, crème fraîche and horseradish in a food processor together with the parsley and the zest and juice of the lemon. Season with lots of pepper. Blend coarsely. Serve with some toasted bread and chunks of lemon.

FISHCAKES

500g potatoes; A knob of butter;
Splash of milk; 4 smoked mackerel fillets;
4 tsp creamed horseradish;
A handful of parsley, chopped;
4 tbsp seasoned flour

1 Boil the potatoes in salted water for about 15 minutes or until tender. Drain, add the butter and milk and mash. Season well and leave to cool.

2 Flake the mackerel fillets. Combine with the mashed potato, horseradish and parsley. Shape handfuls of the mixture into rounds and place in the fridge to firm up.

3 Dust the fishcakes in the seasoned flour and fry in some olive oil, about 5 minutes on each side or until golden and warmed through. Serve.

CRAB, FENNEL AND APPLE

Sliced sourdough

1 apple, core removed

1 fennel bulb

170g tin of white crabmeat

½ a lemon

1 Toast the sourdough. Cut the apple and fennel into matchsticks. Mix the apple and the fennel with the white crabmeat. Top each slice of sourdough with a spoonful of the mixture. Drizzle with a little olive oil and a squeeze of lemon juice.

GARLIC AND TOMATO

Sliced sourdough

½ garlic clove

100g ripe tomatoes, roughly chopped

A handful of basil leaves, torn

1 Toast the sourdough. Drizzle each slice with a little olive oil and rub with half a clove of garlic. Top with the tomatoes and some torn basil leaves.

BROAD BEANS AND PARMESAN

Sliced sourdough

100g broad beans, cooked and peeled

4 tsp créme fraîche

Freshly shaved Parmesan

1 Toast the sourdough. Lightly crush the broad beans. Smear a little crème fraîche onto the slice of sourdough and top with the crushed broad beans, plenty of freshly ground black pepper and Parmesan.

CHICKPEAS WITH TOMATO AND CHOPPED GARLIC

Sliced sourdough

400g tin of chickpeas

150g tomatoes, chopped

1 garlic clove, crushed

A handful of marjoram, chopped

1 Toast the sourdough. Lightly crush the chickpeas using a fork. Mix the chickpeas with the tomatoes, garlic and marjoram. Top the sourdough with a spoonful of the chickpea mixture and serve.

TOASTS

MUSHROOM AND TARRAGON

1 Fry a few handfuls of sliced mushrooms in butter for about 5 minutes or until golden. Season, add a chopped garlic clove and a sprinkling of chopped tarragon. Toast a slice of sourdough and top with the mushroom mixture.

RICOTTA, AVOCADO AND CHILLI

1 Toast a slice of sourdough. Spread over a few spoonfuls of ricotta and top with a some slices of avocado, plenty of salt and a sprinkling of chilli flakes.

RICOTTA AND RED PEPPER

1 Toast a slice of sourdough. Spread over a few spoonfuls of ricotta cheese and top with some freshly roasted or jarred red peppers.

ASPARAGUS AND PARMESAN

1 Toast a slice of sourdough. Cook a handful of asparagus spears in a pan of boiling water for 3 minutes. Drain and refresh under cold running water. Pat dry. Drizzle the toast with a little olive oil. Top with the asparagus and some shavings of Parmesan.

QUICK TOASTS

COURGETTE AND CHILLI

1 Cut a courgette into ribbons. Cook the ribbons in a griddle pan until lightly charred. Toast a slice of sourdough and drizzle with a little olive oil. Top with the griddled courgette and sprinkle with a few chilli flakes and some chopped mint.

GOAT´S CHEESE AND BEETROOT

1 Toast a slice of sourdough. Top with some crumbled goat's cheese, a few slices of cooked beetroot, a handful of peeled orange segments and a sprinkling of chopped mint.

ANCHOVY AND EGG

1 Toast a slice of sourdough. Soft poach an egg in boiling salted water for about 4 minutes. Using a fork, mash a knob of butter with an anchovy fillet and spread onto the toast. Top with the egg.

FENNEL AND SULTANAS

1 Finely slice a fennel bulb and fry in olive oil for 15 minutes or until soft and golden. Add a handful of sultanas and a splash of red wine vinegar to the pan. Stir. Let cool slightly and place on top of the toasted sourdough.

QUICK
TOASTS

WINTER SOUPS

FRENCH ONION

4 large onions, chopped
150g butter
125ml Madeira or medium sweet sherry
1l hot chicken or vegetable stock
2 handfuls of grated Gruyére
2 handfuls of croûtons

1 Place the onions and butter in a pan and sweat over a low heat for about 10 minutes until soft and golden. Add the Madeira. Let bubble until almost evaporated.

2 Add the stock and let simmer for 15 minutes. Scatter with the cheese and croûtons. Season. Serve.

BROCCOLI

1kg broccoli
1 large onion, chopped
2 garlic cloves, finely sliced
A knob of butter
800ml chicken or vegetable stock
200ml double cream
2 handfuls of toasted flaked almonds

1 Slice the broccoli stems and separate from the florets. Set the florets aside. Sweat the stems with the onion and garlic in the butter for 5–8 minutes until soft.

2 Add the stock and bring to the boil. Add the broccoli florets and cook until tender, about 5–8 minutes. Using a hand blender, liquidise the soup and add cream to taste. Season. Reheat in the pan, scatter with almonds and serve.

27

CARROT AND GINGER

1 large onion, diced
2 star anise
3 tsp grated ginger
400g carrots, grated
1 tsp fine sugar
1l chicken or vegetable stock
Single cream, to serve (optional)

1 Sweat the onion, star anise and ginger in olive oil for 10 minutes. Add the carrots, sugar and stock. Cook for 20 minutes.

2 Remove the star anise and using a hand blender, liquidise the soup. Season. Serve, with swirl of cream if you like.

CELERY, PEAR AND STILTON

1 onion, diced;
4–6 celery sticks, diced, extra leaves for garnish;
A large knob of butter; 2 pears;
800ml chicken or vegetable stock;
200ml single cream; 150g Stilton, crumbled

1 Cook the onion and celery gently in the butter for about 10 minutes.

2 Peel, core and chop the pears. Add to the onion and celery, season and pour in the stock. Bring to a simmer and cook for about 15 minutes or until the celery is soft.

3 Using a hand blender, purée and strain back into the pan. Add the cream and the Stilton and warm through until the cheese has melted. Garnish with some celery leaves and serve immediately.

BLINIS

20 blinis
200g smoked salmon
150ml soured cream
50g lumpfish caviar

1 Heat the blinis in the oven for 5 minutes at 180°C/Gas mark 4.

2 Divide the salmon between the blinis, top with a spoonful of the soured cream and a blob of caviar. Serve.

SMOKED SALMON AND ORANGE SALAD

5 oranges
400g smoked salmon
70g watercress
2 x 20g punnets of salad cress
1 fennel bulb, very finely sliced
Olive oil
Lemon wedges, to serve

1 Pare 4 of the oranges to remove all their skin and pith. Slice very thinly and mix in a salad bowl with the salmon, watercress, cress and fennel. Season well.

2 Squeeze the remaining orange, combine the juice with a little oil and dress the salad. Serve with a few lemon wedges.

SALMON PÂTÉ

250g smoked salmon
100g cream cheese
50g crème fraîche
Juice of 1 lemon
Slices of rye bread, to serve

1 Blitz all the ingredients together in a food processor. Season. Toast the rye bread. Spread the pâté on to the toast and serve.

BABY BAKED POTATOES

12 baby potatoes
250g smoked salmon
150ml soured cream
50g lumpfish caviar

1 Rub the potatoes with olive oil and some seasoning. Roast at 200°C/Gas mark 6 for 20–25 minutes.

2 Pinch the potatoes to burst them open or slice an opening using a knife. Divide the salmon between the potatoes, top with a spoonful of the soured cream and a blob of caviar. Serve.

SMOKED SALMON

ONION AND BACON

350g puff pastry; A knob of butter, extra for greasing;
250g onions, finely sliced; 6 rashers of bacon, diced;
150ml double cream; 150ml crème fraîche;
2 eggs, beaten; A large handful of grated cheddar cheese

1 Roll out the pastry. Grease a 24cm metal flan tin and line with pastry, cutting away any excess. Cover with greaseproof paper and fill with baking beans. Bake at 180°C/ Gas mark 4 for 15 minutes. Remove the paper and beans and bake for 10 minutes.

2 Gently sweat the onions in the butter in a covered pan for 30 minutes. In a separate pan, fry the bacon pieces until crispy.

3 Beat together the cream, crème fraîche, eggs and cheese. Season. Add the onion and bacon. Pour into the pastry and bake for 30–40 minutes or until golden. Serve.

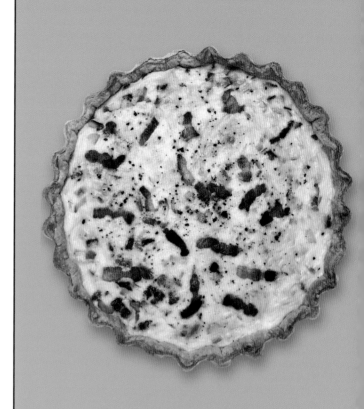

QUICHE

LEEK AND TOMATO

350g puff pastry; A knob of butter, extra for greasing;
2 small leeks, roughly chopped; 150ml double cream;
150ml crème fraîche; 2 eggs, beaten;
A large handful of grated cheddar cheese;
10 cherry tomatoes

1 Roll out the pastry. Grease a 24cm metal flan tin and line with pastry, cutting away any excess. Cover with greaseproof paper and fill with baking beans. Bake at 180°C/ Gas mark 4 for 15 minutes. Remove the paper and beans and bake for 10 minutes.

2 Sweat the leeks in butter over a low heat in a covered pan for 15 minutes, stirring occasionally. Beat the cream, crème fraîche, eggs and cheese. Season. Add the leeks and tomatoes. Pour into the pastry case. Bake for 30–40 minutes or until golden. Serve.

GOAT'S CHEESE AND BROCCOLI

350g puff pastry; A knob of butter, extra for greasing;
4 stems of purple sprouting broccoli; 150ml double cream;
150ml crème fraîche; 2 eggs, beaten;
100g soft goat's cheese

1 Roll out the pastry. Grease a 24cm metal flan tin and line with pastry, cutting away any excess. Cover with greaseproof paper and fill with baking beans. Bake at 180°C/Gas mark 4 for 15 minutes. Remove the paper and beans and bake for 10 minutes.

2 Cook the broccoli in boiling water for 3 minutes. Refresh in cold water and pat dry.

3 Beat together the cream, crème fraîche, eggs and cheese. Season. Add the broccoli. Pour into the pastry case. Bake for 30–40 minutes or until golden. Serve.

31

WATERCRESS AND SMOKED TROUT

350g puff pastry; A knob of butter, extra for greasing;
A large handful of watercress; 150ml double cream;
150ml crème fraîche; 4 eggs, beaten;
200g hot smoked trout, flaked

1 Roll out the pastry. Grease a 24cm metal flan tin and line with pastry, cutting away any excess. Cover with greaseproof paper and fill with baking beans. Bake at 180°C/Gas mark 4 for 15 minutes. Remove the paper and beans and bake for 10 minutes.

2 Melt the butter in a pan and sweat the watercress until wilted, about 1 minute. Beat the cream, crème fraîche and eggs. Season. Stir in the watercress and the trout.

3 Pour into the pastry case. Bake for 30–40 minutes or until golden. Serve.

POACHED WITH GRAPEFRUIT HOLLANDAISE

50ml white wine vinegar; 6 coriander seeds;
2 egg yolks; 150ml olive oil;
Juice of ½ grapefruit; 500g asparagus, trimmed

1 Boil the vinegar and coriander seeds until the liquid has reduced to about 2 tsp. Strain. Transfer the liquid to a heatproof bowl and place over a pan of simmering water – the bowl should not touch the water. Whisk in the egg yolks until pale and creamy and slightly thickened. Slowly add the oil, whisking all the time, until thick and glossy. Season and add a squeeze of grapefruit juice.

2 Boil the asparagus for 3–4 minutes or until tender and serve with the sauce.

GRIDDLED WITH PARMESAN AND BALSAMIC VINEGAR

750g asparagus, trimmed
4 tbsp olive oil
1 tbsp balsamic vinegar
Freshly shaved Parmesan

1 Rub the asparagus with 1 tbsp of the olive oil and place on a hot griddle pan or under the grill, turning occasionally, until cooked – about 5 minutes depending on the thickness.

2 Transfer to a plate. Mix together the remaining oil and the vinegar and drizzle over the asparagus. Scatter with some shavings of Parmesan. Season. Serve.

SOUP

1 large onion; 2 celery sticks; 500g asparagus, trimmed;
1l hot chicken or vegetable stock; 75g Parma ham

1 Dice the onion and celery and cook gently in oil for about 5 minutes or until soft. Cut off the tips of the asparagus and reserve. Roughly chop the stems and add to the saucepan. Cook for about 5 minutes.

2 Add the stock and simmer, uncovered, for 5 minutes or until the asparagus is cooked. Meanwhile, blanch the asparagus tips for about 2 minutes in boiling water. Wrap in Parma ham and fry in hot oil for 1–2 minutes or until golden.

3 Using a hand blender, blitz the soup, season. Serve drizzled with oil and the wrapped asparagus tips scattered over.

ASPARAGUS AND STILTON TART

20 asparagus spears, trimmed
300g puff pastry
Butter, for greasing
250g Stilton or other blue cheese, crumbled

1 Preheat the oven to 200°C/Gas mark 6. Cook the asparagus in salted boiling water for about 3 minutes or until just tender.

2 Roll the pastry out into a rectangle large enough to comfortably accommodate the asparagus. Score a line 2.5cm in from the edge, all the way round, and place onto a greased baking tray.

3 Lay the asparagus on the pastry and top with the Stilton. Bake for 10 minutes or until puffed and golden. Serve.

ASPARAGUS

CRAB AND AVOCADO

8 eggs, separated
150g cooked white crabmeat
1 ripe avocado, peeled and diced
1 tbsp chopped tarragon
A knob of butter

1 Beat the yolks and season. Whisk the whites in a clean, dry bowl until they form soft peaks. Use a metal spoon to carefully fold the yolks into the whites. Fold in the crab, avocado and tarragon.

2 Melt the butter in a non-stick frying pan over a high heat. Pour in the egg mixture and cook for 2 minutes. Place the pan under the grill and cook for a further minute to brown. Serve.

OMELETTE

PLAIN

8 eggs
Splash of milk
A knob of butter

1 Heat a non-stick frying pan over a high heat. Lightly beat the eggs in a bowl with a splash of milk. Season. Heat the butter in a frying pan and when it starts foaming pour in the eggs. Season. Using a plastic spatula, pull the edges of the omelette to the centre and shake the pan to distribute any uncooked egg. Cook for a further 1–2 minutes then remove from the heat.

2 Add a filling if you wish (ham, grated cheese, cooked mushrooms, smoked salmon, etc.). Fold over both edges to overlap at the centre and serve.

PEA, FETA AND MINT

150g frozen peas, defrosted
8 eggs, beaten
100g feta, crumbled
A handful of mint, chopped
A large knob of butter

1 Combine all the ingredients (except for the butter) in a bowl. Season well. Heat the butter in a non-stick frying pan until foaming. Pour in the egg and cheese mixture and cook until the bottom is set, about 3 minutes. Place under a hot grill for 1 minute to set the top.

SPANISH

1 onion, sliced; 1 red or green pepper;
600g cooked new potatoes, thickly sliced; 8 eggs, beaten

1 Heat some oil in a large frying pan, add the onion and cook gently without colouring, about 5 minutes. Peel the pepper using a swivel peeler, cut into slices and add to the onion. Add the potatoes and cook until the peppers are soft and the potatoes have coloured, about 10 minutes.

2 Transfer the onions, peppers and potatoes to a bowl. Add the beaten eggs. Mix well. Season. In a clean non-stick frying pan, add some more oil and pour in the egg mixture. Cook until the bottom is set, about 3 minutes, then place under a hot grill until the top has set, about 1 minute. Serve.

WARM CHICKEN AND BABY GEM

3–4 chicken breasts; 100g butter;
4 anchovy fillets; 3 garlic cloves, chopped;
3 baby gem lettuces, torn; Zest and juice of 1 lemon

1 Cook the chicken breasts in the oven or under the grill for about 15 minutes or until cooked through. Allow to rest for 5 minutes, then cut into 1cm wide slices.

2 Meanwhile, melt the butter in a large saucepan. Add the anchovies and cook gently, stirring with a wooden spoon to break them up. Once dissolved, add the garlic and cook for 2–3 minutes without browning.

3 Add the lettuce leaves and toss in the sauce for 1 minute or until slightly wilted. Remove from the heat. Add the chicken, zest and a squeeze of lemon juice. Season. Serve.

36

LENTILS WITH BUTTERNUT SQUASH AND RED ONIONS

1 squash, peeled and cut; 2 red onions, cut into chunks;
1 tsp cumin seeds; 100g lentils; 1 bay leaf;
2 rashers of smoked bacon; 3 tbsp natural yoghurt;
2 tbsp white wine vinegar; 1 tbsp olive oil;
Juice and zest of ½ lemon; A handful of parsley, torn

1 Place the squash, onions and cumin in a roasting tin with some oil. Cook at 180°C/Gas mark 4 for 40 minutes or until soft.

2 Meanwhile, place the lentils in a saucepan and just cover with cold water. Add the bay leaf and bacon. Simmer, covered, for 20–25 minutes. Add more water if needed. Once cooked, drain and discard the bacon and bay. Combine with the squash and onions.

3 Mix the yoghurt, vinegar and olive oil. Stir into the lentils with the lemon zest, juice and seasoning. Sprinkle with parsley. Serve.

ORANGE, FENNEL AND WATERCRESS

1 fennel bulb; 1 red onion;
Red wine vinegar; 3 small oranges;
2 tbsp olive oil; 4 large handfuls of watercress;
200g goat's cheese

1 Slice the fennel and red onion very thinly. Rinse the onion in water and cover with vinegar for 20 minutes. With a sharp knife, cut the skin and all the pith from 2 of the oranges. Slice into thin discs. Drain the onion, reserving some of the liquid. Place the fennel, onion and orange into a salad bowl. Season.

2 Zest and juice the remaining orange. Whisk with the oil and 2 tbsp of the onion vinegar. Dress the watercress. Serve with slices of the goat's cheese.

GORGONZOLA AND SPICED PEAR

250ml red wine; 100ml red wine vinegar; 1 whole chilli;
150g brown sugar; 1 cinnamon stick; 6 cloves;
1 tsp juniper; 2 star anise; 4 Conference pears, peeled;
75g walnuts; 2 chicory heads, leaves separated;
3 tbsp olive oil; 1 tbsp balsamic vinegar;
½ tsp Dijon mustard; 200g Gorgonzola, crumbled

1 Mix the wine, vinegar, chilli, sugar and spices in a saucepan large enough to fit the pears. Bring to the boil. Add the whole pears and cook gently, about 20 minutes, until soft when pierced with a knife. Allow to cool.

2 Toast the nuts for about 5 minutes in a dry pan, tossing regularly. Place in a bowl with the chicory. Slice the pears. Mix the oil, vinegar and mustard and dress the leaves. Add the Gorgonzola and pears. Season. Serve.

WINTER SALADS

SCRAMBLED EGGS

PLAIN

8 eggs

A large knob of butter, extra if desired

Crème fraîche (optional)

Slices of toast, to serve

1 Lightly beat the eggs. Melt the butter in a pan. When the butter starts foaming, add the eggs, season and stir with a spatula over a gentle heat until it forms thick curds.

2 Add a dollop of crème fraîche or some more butter to the eggs if you like and serve with the toast.

MEXICAN EGGS

2 tbsp olive oil; 1 onion, finely chopped;

1 chilli, finely chopped; 2 garlic cloves, finely chopped;

1 green pepper, diced; 4 tomatoes, quartered;

8 eggs, beaten; A large knob of butter;

A large handful of coriander, chopped; Flatbread, to serve

1 Heat the oil in a large pan and gently fry the onion, chilli, garlic and green pepper for 10–15 minutes or until caramelised. Add the tomatoes and cook for 2–3 minutes more.

2 Scramble the eggs following step 1 of the Plain recipe. Cook until the eggs are slightly runny. Fold in the onion and chilli mixture, scatter over the coriander and serve with a warmed flatbread.

SMOKED HADDOCK

1 fillet of smoked haddock, about 300g;

250ml milk; 1 bay leaf; 6 peppercorns;

8 eggs; A large knob of butter;

A handful of parsley, chopped

1 Place the haddock in a pan with the milk, bay leaf and the peppercorns. Bring to the boil and simmer for 2–3 minutes or until the haddock is cooked. Drain through a sieve and reserve 100ml of the liquid. Discard the skin from the fish.

2 Lightly beat the eggs with the reserved milk. Don't add any seasoning. Make scrambled eggs as step 1 of the Plain recipe. Top with the flaked fish and a sprinkling of parsley before serving.

CREAM CHEESE AND CHIVES

8 eggs

A large knob of butter

100g cream cheese

2 tbsp crème fraîche

A handful of chives, chopped

1 Scramble the eggs by following step 1 of the Plain recipe.

2 In a small bowl, use a metal spoon to beat the cream cheese with the crème fraîche to soften. Fold in the eggs. Season, sprinkle over the chives and serve.

MAIN

DISHES

LEEK AND MUSHROOM FRICASSEE

1 leek, sliced; A large handful of mushrooms, sliced;
A few sprigs of thyme; 1 bay leaf; 300ml chicken stock;
300ml double cream; 4 chicken breasts

1 Heat an oiled frying pan. Add the leek, mushrooms, thyme and bay leaf and cook for about 10 minutes or until the mushrooms are coloured and the leeks are soft.

2 Add the stock and gently boil for about 10 minutes or until reduced by half. Add the cream and cook for another 5 minutes or until thickened. Season.

3 Meanwhile, season the chicken breasts and fry in a separate oiled pan, about 3 minutes on each side or until coloured. Transfer to a 200°C/Gas mark 6 oven for a further 5 minutes or until cooked. Serve with the leek and mushroom sauce spooned over.

ASIAN SOUP

1l chicken stock; 2 lemongrass stalks, bruised;
1 small knob of ginger, roughly sliced;
2 red chillies, one finely sliced;
2 shallots, roughly sliced;
2 tsp fine sugar; A handful of mushrooms, sliced;
4 chicken breasts, sliced; Juice of 1 lime;
2 tbsp soy sauce; A handful of coriander, chopped

1 Add the stock, lemongrass, ginger, whole chilli, shallots and sugar to a pan. Simmer for 10 minutes. Strain, reserving the stock.

2 Bring the stock back up to a simmer and poach the mushrooms and chicken for 5–8 minutes or until cooked. Add the lime juice and soy sauce to taste. Scatter with the coriander and the sliced chillies. Check the seasoning and serve.

THAI STIR-FRY

Groundnut oil; 2 large chicken breasts, diced;
200g medium rice noodles; 2 handfuls of mangetout;
1 large courgette, cut into strips; 1 red pepper, sliced;
A few spring onions, sliced;
A handful of coriander leaves, chopped;
2 tbsp finely grated ginger; Juice of 1 lime;
2 tbsp sesame oil; 2 tbsp Thai fish sauce;
1 red chilli, deseeded and finely chopped;
1 tbsp soft brown sugar

1 Heat a splash of oil in a wok and cook the chicken for 5 minutes or until almost cooked. Place the noodles in boiling water for a few minutes to warm through. Drain.

2 Add more oil to the wok and stir-fry all the vegetables for 3 minutes. Add the noodles and coriander and cook for 1 minute. Mix the ginger, lime, sesame oil, fish sauce, chilli and sugar. Pour over the stir-fry. Serve.

TARRAGON AND YOGHURT

4 skinless chicken breasts
4 tbsp natural yoghurt
A large handful of tarragon, finely chopped
2 tbsp Worcestershire sauce
Mixed salad leaves, to serve

1 Slice each chicken breast in half lengthways, creating two escalopes. Mix together the remaining ingredients with some seasoning. Cover all of the chicken and leave to marinate for at least 30 minutes.

2 Heat a grill or ridged pan and cook the chicken for about 3 minutes on each side, or until cooked all the way through. Season. Serve on a bed of salad.

CHICKEN BREASTS

PUFF PASTRY

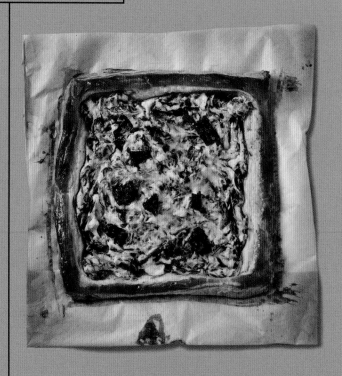

ONION AND ANCHOVY TART

100g butter; 1kg onions, finely sliced;
½ tsp dried thyme; 300g puff pastry;
12 anchovy fillets;
A large handful of pitted black olives;
1 egg, beaten

1 Melt the butter in a saucepan, add the onions, thyme and seasoning and cook very gently for about an hour, stirring often, until the onions are sweet and caramelised.

2 Roll out the puff pastry until 35x35cm square and score a line 2cm in from each outside edge. Cover the inside square with the onions and dot with anchovies and olives. Brush the exposed edge with some egg.

3 Cook at 200°C/Gas mark 6 for about 20 minutes or until golden. Serve.

MUSHROOM AND CHEESE PARCELS

8 mushrooms, sliced; 300g puff pastry;
150g cream cheese with herbs; 4 tomatoes, sliced;
1 egg, beaten

1 Fry the mushrooms in a little olive oil until softened, about 5 minutes. Drain on some kitchen paper.

2 Roll out the puff pastry into a 30x30cm square. Cut into four smaller squares. Divide the cheese, tomatoes and mushrooms between the pastry and place in the middle of the squares. Fold the pastry over the filling to form triangles. Brush the inside edges with a little egg and pinch to seal.

3 Brush the top of the triangles with the remaining egg. Cook at 200°C/Gas mark 6 for 15 minutes or until they are puffed and golden. Serve.

HAM AND CHEESE PARCELS

300g puff pastry
2 tsp Dijon mustard
8 slices of good-quality ham
150g Gruyére, sliced
1 egg, beaten

1 Roll the puff pastry out into a 30x30cm square. Cut into four smaller squares. Spread the mustard over the slices of ham. Divide the ham and cheese equally, placing in the middle of each square. Fold the pastry over the filling to form triangles. Brush the inside edges with egg and pinch to seal.

2 Brush the top of the triangles with the remaining egg. Cook at 200°C/Gas mark 6 for 15 minutes or until they are puffed and golden. Serve.

SPINACH AND RICOTTA TART

300g frozen spinach, defrosted; 250g ricotta;
A large handful of grated Parmesan;
A pinch of nutmeg; Zest of 1 lemon;
A handful of sun-dried tomatoes, chopped;
320g puff pastry; 1 egg, beaten

1 Squeeze the water out of the spinach. Combine with the ricotta, Parmesan, nutmeg, lemon zest and tomatoes. Season.

2 Roll out the pastry to form a 30x30cm square. Score a line 2cm in from each outside edge. Fill the centre square with the spinach mixture. Brush the exposed edge with some egg.

3 Cook at 200°C/Gas mark 6 for about 20 minutes or until golden. Serve.

ASIAN

120ml mirin or sweet cooking wine; 4 tbsp soy sauce;
2 tbsp honey; 2.5cm knob of ginger, grated;
4 salmon fillets, skinned; 4 tbsp rice vinegar;
Cooked plain rice and stir-fried vegetables, to serve

1 Combine the mirin, soy, honey and ginger and pour over the salmon. Leave to marinate for at least 20 minutes.

2 Heat a dash of oil in a large frying pan. Cook the salmon fillets for about 5 minutes on each side, turning only once.

3 Remove the salmon from the pan. Add the marinade to the pan along with the rice vinegar. Boil for 2–3 minutes or until slightly reduced and syrupy. Serve with plain boiled rice and some stir-fried vegetables.

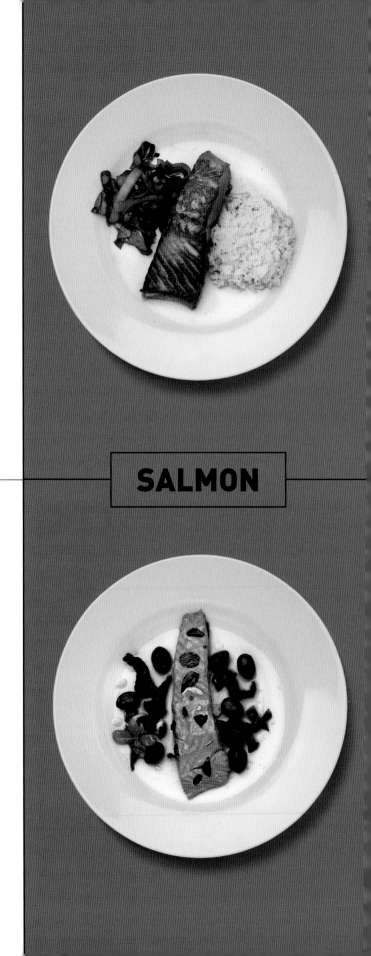

SALMON

ITALIAN

4 salmon fillets, skinned
8 sun-dried tomatoes in oil, chopped
A handful of pitted black olives
2 garlic cloves, thinly sliced
A few basil leaves

1 Drizzle a large ovenproof dish with olive oil. Lay the salmon fillets in a single layer and scatter over the tomatoes, olives and garlic. Season and cover with a lid or tin foil.

2 Cook in the oven at 180°C/Gas mark 4 for 15–20 minutes. Garnish with a few basil leaves and serve.

INDIAN

1 tbsp tandoori paste
150ml natural yoghurt
4 salmon fillets, skinned
Plain rice and mango and parsley salad, to serve

1 Mix the paste with the yoghurt in a small bowl. Spread over the salmon and leave to marinate for at least 30 minutes.

2 Grill under a medium heat for 5–10 minutes, turning once, or until cooked through. Serve with some plain boiled rice and a mango salad.

ENGLISH

75g unsalted butter; 1 large onion, thinly sliced;
6 rashers of smoked bacon, diced;
A handful of frozen peas, defrosted; 200ml chicken stock;
1 tbsp horseradish; 1 tbsp olive oil; 4 salmon fillets

1 Melt a knob of the butter in a saucepan and add the onion and bacon. Cook for 5 minutes or until the onions are soft and the bacon has browned. Add the peas and enough stock to cover. Bring to the boil and cook for 5 minutes. Stir in the remaining butter and horseradish. Season. Keep warm.

2 Heat the oil in a large frying pan. Season the salmon and cook skin-side down for 5 minutes until the skin is crispy. Turn the fish over and cook for a further minute. Serve on top of the onion and pea sauce.

SPICY

800g minced beef; A handful of breadcrumbs;
1 red chilli, finely chopped; 1 tsp ground coriander;
1 tsp ground cumin; 1 egg; Burger buns, torn lettuce
leaves, tomato slices, mayonnaise and mustard, to serve

1 Mix together the beef, breadcrumbs, chilli, coriander, cumin and egg in a bowl. Season well and shape into four equal burger shapes.

2 Brush each burger with some olive oil and cook over a medium heat in a griddle or frying pan for 4–5 minutes on each side.

3 Serve in a bun with some lettuce, tomato, mayonnaise and mustard.

LAMB

800g minced lamb
1 red onion, finely chopped
1 tsp finely chopped rosemary
A handful of mint, chopped
Pitta bread, fried onions, a handful of chopped parsley
and houmous, to serve

1 Mix together the lamb, onion, rosemary and mint in a bowl. Season well and shape into four equal burger shapes.

2 Brush each burger with olive oil and cook over a medium heat in a griddle or frying pan for 4–5 minutes on each side.

3 Serve the burgers in a warmed pitta bread with some fried onions, parsley and a dollop of houmous.

VEGGIE

1 large onion, chopped; 2 garlic cloves, crushed;
1 tsp cumin seeds; 2 tsp coriander seeds, crushed;
A pinch of dried chilli flakes; 2 x 400g tins of chickpeas;
1 tbsp tahini; Zest of 1 lemon; 25g parsley, chopped;
3–4 handfuls of breadcrumbs; 1 egg, beaten; Flour; Salad

1 Heat some olive oil in a pan. Fry the onion and garlic over a gentle heat until soft and slightly caramelised, about 10–15 minutes. Add the cumin, coriander and chilli and cook for 1 minute then remove from the heat.

2 Coarsely blend the chickpeas. Season well (add lots of salt). Mix in the onion, tahini, zest, parsley and breadcrumbs and enough beaten egg to bind the mixture.

3 Shape into four patties. Dust with flour and fry in oil for 5 minutes on each side, or until golden and warm. Serve with a salad.

CLASSIC

800g minced beef; A handful of breadcrumbs;
1 egg, beaten; A handful of parsley, finely chopped;
Burger buns, torn lettuce leaves, tomato slices,
onion slices, gherkins, mustard and a lemon wedge,
to serve

1 Mix together the beef, breadcrumbs, egg and parsley in a bowl. Season well and shape into four equal burger shapes.

2 Brush each burger with olive oil and cook over a medium heat in a griddle or frying pan for 4–5 minutes on each side.

3 Serve in a burger bun with some lettuce, tomato slices, onion slices, gherkins, a dollop of mustard and a wedge of lemon.

BURGERS

ROAST CHICKEN

LEMON

A knob of butter; 1 chicken, about 1.8kg; 1 lemon;
4 garlic cloves, whole and crushed;
250ml white wine

1 Rub the butter over the whole bird. Roll the lemon on the worktop to loosen the juices, halve and pierce all over using a sharp knife. Place the lemon and garlic in the cavity of the chicken. Season well.

2 Roast at 200°C/Gas mark 6 for 1 hour. Once the skin is golden brown and the juices run clear when the thickest part is pierced with a knife, remove from the oven and leave to rest covered with tin foil. Meanwhile, make the gravy by simmering the cooking juices in the roasting tray with the wine until reduced. Scrape the burnt bits at the bottom with a wooden spoon to release more flavour.

SPICED

1 chicken, about 1.8kg; 1 onion; 2 garlic cloves, crushed;
3 lemongrass stalks; 1 red chilli;
5cm knob of ginger, grated; Juice of 2 limes;
1 tbsp fish sauce; A handful of coriander, with stems;
1 tbsp brown sugar

1 Cut deep slits into the chicken thighs, leg and breast. Blitz all the ingredients (except the chicken) in a food processor and rub all over the chicken, and well into the slits. Leave to marinate for at least 2 hours.

2 Wrap the chicken with the marinade in some tin foil and place on a roasting tray. Roast at 200°C/Gas mark 6 for 1 hour and 15 minutes. Remove the tin foil, baste the chicken with its juices and cook for a further 15 minutes until the skin is browned and the juices run clear when pierced with a knife.

PROSCIUTTO AND ROSEMARY

70g prosciutto
A few sprigs of rosemary
A large knob of butter
Zest of 1 lemon
1 chicken, about 1.8kg

1 Roughly chop the prosciutto and finely chop the rosemary. Mix with the butter and the lemon zest. Loosen the skin around the top breast of the chicken and work the butter mixture into the space. Smear any leftovers over the top of the bird.

2 Roast in the oven at 200°C/Gas mark 6 for 1 hour, basting the chicken with its juices occasionally. The chicken is done when the skin is golden, and the juices run clear when the thickest part is pierced with a knife.

BALSAMIC VINEGAR

1 lemon; 4 garlic cloves, whole and crushed;
1 chicken, about 1.8kg; A sprig of rosemary;
4 tbsp extra virgin olive oil; 4 tbsp balsamic vinegar;
A handful of oregano, chopped

1 Roll the lemon on the worktop to loosen the juices and pierce all over with a sharp knife. Place the lemon and garlic in the chicken cavity with the rosemary. Drizzle the top with olive oil and season well.

2 Roast in the oven at 180°C/Gas mark 4 for 40 minutes. Pour over the balsamic vinegar and cook for a further 30 minutes. The chicken is done when the skin is golden, and the juices run clear when the thickest part is pierced with a knife. Serve the chicken with a sprinkling of oregano and the balsamic gravy from the pan.

ANCHOVY AND CAPER

8 lamb chops
100g butter
4 anchovy fillets, mashed
2 garlic cloves, crushed
1 tbsp capers
1 tbsp chopped parsley
Juice of 1 lemon
Cooked puy lentils, to serve

1 Season the chops. Cook in a hot pan, fatty edge down, for 5 minutes to render the fat. Fry for 3 minutes on each side of the meat.

2 Drain the fat from the pan, reduce the heat and add the butter, anchovies, garlic, capers and parsley. Cook for about 2 minutes, spooning the butter mixture over the chops. Mix in the lemon juice. Serve with puy lentils.

LAMB CHOPS

SAGE AND BUTTER

8 lamb chops
A large knob of butter
8 sage leaves
New potatoes and broad beans, to serve

1 Season the chops. Cook in a hot pan, fatty edge down, for 5 minutes to render the fat. Fry for 3 minutes on each side of the meat.

2 Drain the fat from the pan, reduce the heat and add the butter. Once it starts foaming, add the sage leaves and spoon the butter over the chops for a further minute. Serve with new potatoes and broad beans.

HOUMOUS AND ONION

1 large onion, finely sliced
A pinch of ground cumin
A pinch of ground cinnamon
200g houmous
8 lamb chops
2 tbsp pine nuts
Mixed salad, to serve

1 Fry the onion in oil, stirring occasionally, until golden, about 10 minutes. Add the cumin and cinnamon and cook for a further minute. Let cool and stir into the houmous.

2 Season the chops. Place under a hot grill. Cook for 6 minutes, turning halfway through cooking. Toast the pine nuts for 2–3 minutes in a dry frying pan.

3 Serve the chops with a dollop of houmous, a scattering of pine nuts and a salad.

MINT AND PEAS

8 lamb chops; 4 shallots, quartered;
2 carrots, cut into batons; 125ml white wine;
250ml chicken stock; 4 handfuls of frozen peas;
A large knob of butter; 1 baby gem lettuce, shredded;
A large handful of mint, shredded

1 Season the chops. Cook in a hot pan, fatty edge down, for 5 minutes to render the fat. Fry for 3 minutes on each side of the meat. Remove the chops and keep warm.

2 Drain the fat from the pan. Add the shallots and carrots. Cook for 2–3 minutes, add the wine and bubble for 3 minutes or until reduced. Add the stock, peas and butter. Cook for 6 minutes or until the peas are tender.

3 Add the lettuce and take off the heat. Add the mint and season. Serve the lamb chops on top of the vegetables.

FETA AND SUN-DRIED TOMATO

200g couscous
250ml boiling chicken or vegetable stock
2 tbsp sun-dried tomatoes in oil, chopped
200g feta, crumbled
A handful of pine nuts
A handful of basil, chopped

1 Just cover the couscous with the stock and leave to stand for 10 minutes.

2 Fluff up the couscous with a fork, stir in the sun-dried tomatoes, feta, pine nuts and basil. Season. Serve.

BROAD BEANS, MINT AND YOGHURT

200g couscous; 250ml boiling chicken stock;
200g Greek yoghurt; 1 garlic clove, crushed;
2 tbsp extra virgin olive oil; 2 tsp sumac;
4 handfuls of broad beans; 2 handfuls of mint, chopped

1 Just cover the couscous with the stock and leave to stand for 10 minutes. Fluff up the cooked couscous with a fork.

2 Mix the yoghurt, garlic, oil and sumac. Season well.

3 Meanwhile, cook the broad beans in a pan of boiling water for about 6 minutes or until tender. Drain.

4 Top the couscous with the yoghurt, beans and mint. Serve.

ROASTED VEGETABLES

1 aubergine; 2 courgettes; 1 red pepper;
6 tomatoes; 2 red onions; 1 fennel bulb;
4 garlic cloves, peel left on and crushed;
250g couscous; 250ml boiling vegetable stock;
25g butter; 2 tbsp harissa paste; 1 tbsp chopped parsley

1 Cut all the vegetables into equal-sized chunks. Drizzle with oil and scatter over the garlic cloves. Roast at 190°C/Gas mark 5 for 30 minutes.

2 Meanwhile, just cover the couscous with the stock. Leave for 10 minutes. Fluff the couscous with a fork. Season well and stir in the butter and the harissa. Mix in the roasted vegetables and scatter over the parsley.

COUSCOUS SALAD

200g couscous; 250ml boiling vegetable stock;
12 cherry tomatoes, halved; ½ cucumber, in chunks;
40g sultanas; 40g toasted flaked almonds;
Zest and juice of 2 lemons; 6 tbsp olive oil;
1 tbsp each of chopped mint, basil and parsley

1 Just cover the couscous with the stock and leave to stand for 10 minutes. Fluff up the cooked couscous with a fork. Leave to cool.

2 Mix in all of the remaining ingredients. Add plenty of salt. Serve.

COUSCOUS

STEAK

STEAK BURGER

1 small onion
A handful of parsley
500g coarsely minced rib-eye steak
4 brioche buns
Torn lettuce leaves and sliced pickled gherkins, to serve

1 Finely chop the onion and parsley and add to the mince. Season well. Divide into 4 equal balls and flatten to about 2cm thick.

2 Heat a frying or grill pan until smoking hot. Brush the burgers with a little oil and add more salt. Cook for about 6 minutes, turning regularly, until charred but still pink on the inside.

3 Toast the brioche bun. Serve the burger in the bun with a few lettuce leaves and a few gherkins.

TARTARE

800g fillet or sirloin
2 small shallots, finely chopped
4 tbsp capers, chopped
2 tbsp chopped parsley
2 tbsp ketchup
2 tbsp Worcestershire sauce
2 tbsp Dijon mustard
4 egg yolks
Tabasco sauce and pickled gherkins, to serve

1 Mince the steak. Mix with everything apart from the yolks, Tabasco and gherkins. Season well.

2 Divide the mixture equally into four. Top each portion with a raw egg yolk. Serve with some Tabasco, olive oil and a gherkin on the side.

RARE

4 fillet steaks, about 2.5cm thick
Groundnut oil
Mixed salad, to serve

1 Bring the steaks up to room temperature. Heat a large frying or griddle pan over a high heat until it is smoking hot. Brush the steaks on both sides with the groundnut oil and season well. Place the steak in the pan and, without moving it, fry for 2 minutes. Flip over and cook for a further minute.

2 Place on a rack, cover with foil and leave to rest for 6 minutes in a warm place. Serve immediately.

MEDIUM-RARE

4 sirloin steaks, about 2.5cm thick;
Groundnut oil; Chips and sauces, to serve

1 Bring the steaks up to room temperature. Heat a large frying or griddle pan over a high heat until it is smoking hot. Brush the steaks on both sides with the groundnut oil and season well. Place the steak in the pan and, without moving it, fry for 2½ minutes. Flip over and cook for a further 2 minutes.

2 Place on a rack, cover with foil and rest for 5 minutes in a warm place. Serve.

For medium: 3½ minutes; turn; 3 minutes; rest for 4 minutes.
For well-done: 4½ minutes; turn; 4 minutes; rest for 1 minute.

MUSHROOM

1 While the steaks are resting, add oil to the steak pan. Fry 1 chopped onion for 3 minutes, then add 2 crushed garlic cloves and 150g sliced mushrooms and cook for 4 minutes. Add 1 tbsp brandy and cook for 1 minute. Add 150ml crème fraîche and some chopped tarragon and lemon juice. Serve on top of the steak.

CHIMICHURRI

1 Place 60ml olive oil, 2 garlic cloves, 1 tsp crushed chilli flakes, ½ tsp paprika, 1 tbsp balsamic vinegar and 1 tbsp each of chopped oregano, thyme and parsley in a blender and blitz. Drizzle over the cooked steak to serve.

PEPPERCORN

1 While the steaks are resting, add oil to the steak pan. Fry 1 chopped onion for 3 minutes, then add 2 crushed garlic cloves. Add 2 tbsp peppercorns and 2 tbsp brandy. Cook for another minute, add 150ml crème fraîche, warm through and serve on top of the steak.

ANCHOVY BUTTER

1 Blitz 6 anchovy fillets and 1 garlic clove to a pulp in a blender. Add 1 tbsp chopped parsley, 2 tsp capers, the zest of 1 lemon, 100g softened butter and some black pepper. Mix together. Serve on top of the steak or chill or freeze until needed.

STEAK BUTTERS AND SAUCES

BÉARNAISE

1 Boil 2 sliced shallots, 1 tsp peppercorns, 4 tbsp white wine vinegar, 1 tbsp water and 3 tarragon sprigs until reduced. Cool. Strain. Place 3 egg yolks to a bowl and set over boiling water. Add the vinegar and whisk for 10 minutes until creamy. Take off the heat. Whisk in 200g melted butter. Season. Add lemon juice, chopped tarragon and serve.

CHILLI

1 Mix together 100g softened butter, 2 finely chopped red chillies, 2 tsp chopped coriander and zest of ½ a lime. Season and serve over the steak or chill or freeze until it is needed.

PORCINI

1 Place 50g dried porcini in a saucepan with 2 crushed garlic cloves and just enough water to cover. Bring to the boil and simmer until about 2 tsp of liquid remains. Let cool and then chop the porcini. Combine the porcini with 100g softened butter. Season well. Serve with the steak or chill or freeze until needed.

BLUE CHEESE

1 Crumble 100g Stilton and mix with 100g soft unsalted butter, 1 tsp Dijon mustard, 2 tsp chopped parsley and a pinch of celery salt. Combine all the ingredients. Serve on top of the steak or chill or freeze until needed.

STEAK
BUTTERS
AND SAUCES

BEEF IN RED WINE

750g diced stewing beef; 1 large onion, chopped;
2 celery sticks, chopped; 2 carrots, sliced;
6 anchovy fillets; 1 bay leaf; 500ml red wine;
500ml chicken stock; A handful of parsley, chopped

1 Heat oil in a casserole dish. Season the meat and seal by browning all over, in 2 or 3 batches. Remove the beef and keep warm.

2 Add more oil to the dish and gently cook the vegetables until soft, about 10 minutes. Add the anchovies and bay leaf and cook for another 2–3 minutes, stirring until the fillets have broken down.

3 Add the wine and stock and boil until reduced by half. Add the beef, season and bring to the boil. Cook, covered, for 2–3 hours in the oven at 150°C/Gas mark 2. Sprinkle with the parsley and serve.

CASSEROLES

PORK WITH FENNEL AND APPLE

750g diced pork shoulder; 1 onion, chopped;
2 fennel bulbs, thickly sliced and leaves reserved;
3 bay leaves; 1 cooking apple, core removed and sliced;
250ml cider; 250ml chicken stock

1 Heat oil in a casserole dish. Season the meat and seal by browning all over, in 2 or 3 batches. Remove the pork and keep warm.

2 Add more oil to the dish and gently cook the onion and fennel until soft, about 10 minutes. Add the bay leaf and apple and cook for 3–4 minutes, stirring occasionally.

3 Add the cider and stock and return the pork to the dish. Bring to a simmer and cook, covered, for 3 hours in the oven at 150°C/Gas mark 2. Sprinkle with some chopped fennel leaves if you like.

CHICKEN WITH MUSHROOMS AND TARRAGON

1 small chicken, jointed into 6; 4 tbsp plain flour;
200g smoked bacon, diced; 12 shallots, peeled;
250ml white wine; 2 tbsp Dijon mustard;
500ml chicken stock; 2 handfuls of button mushrooms;
100ml double cream; A handful of tarragon, chopped

1 Dust the chicken in flour. Heat some oil in a casserole dish and brown the chicken, in 2 or 3 batches. Remove and keep warm.

2 Add more oil to the dish and cook the bacon and shallots until coloured. Add the wine and reduce by half. Add the mustard and stock and return the chicken to the dish. Simmer, covered, for 40 minutes. Add the mushrooms and cook for 20 more minutes.

3 Remove the chicken. Reduce the sauce. Add cream, tarragon and the chicken and warm through. Serve.

MOROCCAN LAMB

750g diced lamb neck; 1 large onion, chopped;
2 celery sticks, chopped; 2 carrots, chopped;
2 tsp ground cinnamon; 2 tsp ground cumin;
A pinch of chilli flakes; A knob of ginger, grated;
400g tin of tomatoes; 2 handfuls of dried prunes;
500ml chicken stock; A handful of parsley, chopped

1 Heat oil in a casserole dish. Season the meat and seal by browning all over, in 2 or 3 batches. Remove the lamb and keep warm.

2 Add more oil to the dish and cook the vegetables for 10 minutes until soft. Add the spices and cook for another 3–4 minutes.

3 Add the tomatoes, prunes and stock. Season. Return the meat to the dish and bring to the boil. Cook, covered, for about 2 hours in the oven at 150°C/Gas mark 2. Sprinkle with the parsley.

FROZEN PEAS

PEA AND CHORIZO

2 small onions, chopped; 75g chorizo, chopped;
1 tsp paprika; 125ml white wine;
250ml chicken stock; 250g frozen peas;
A large knob of butter;
2 eggs, hard boiled, broken into pieces

1 Heat a dash of olive oil in a pan. Add the onions and chorizo and cook gently until soft, about 10 minutes. Add the paprika and cook for another minute.

2 Turn up the heat, add the wine and allow to bubble and reduce for about 3 minutes. Add the stock, bring to the boil and add the peas. Simmer for 6 minutes until tender.

3 Stir in the butter and scatter over the eggs. Season. Serve.

PEA, BASIL AND BACON FRITTATA

2 shallots, chopped
6 rashers of smoked bacon, chopped
200g frozen peas
8 eggs, beaten
A handful of basil, torn

1 In a large ovenproof frying pan, fry the shallots and bacon gently until the onions are soft and the bacon is starting to brown, about 10 minutes. Cook the peas in boiling salted water for about 5 minutes or until almost ready. Drain.

2 Add the eggs and the peas to the pan. Season and stir together. Sprinkle over the basil and cook over a gentle heat for about 5 minutes. Place the pan under the grill and cook for a further 5 minutes or until cooked through and golden. Serve.

63

PEA RISOTTO

1 onion, chopped; 350g risotto rice; 250ml white wine;
1¼l hot chicken or vegetable stock; 250g frozen peas;
A large knob of butter; A handful of tarragon, chopped;
A handful of grated Parmesan

1 Heat a dash of oil in a pan and cook the onion for 3–5 minutes until soft but not yet coloured. Add the rice and stir for 1 minute. Add the wine and cook for 2 minutes before adding the stock, one ladleful at a time. Stir until absorbed before adding the next spoonful.

2 About 12 minutes after adding the first ladle of stock, stir in the peas. Continue adding more of the stock until the rice and the peas are cooked.

3 Add the butter, tarragon and Parmesan. Season. Serve.

CHILLED PEA SOUP

2 celery sticks
2 garlic cloves
2–3 spring onions, white parts only
2 large knobs of butter
1l chicken or vegetable stock
500g frozen peas
200ml milk
4 tbsp crème fraîche

1 Slice the celery, garlic and the whites of the onions. Heat the butter in a pan and gently cook the celery, garlic and onion until soft but not coloured, about 10 minutes.

2 Add the stock and bring to the boil. Add the peas and cook until tender, about 6 minutes. Remove from the heat, add the milk and blitz with a hand blender. Season well. Chill. Serve with a dollop of crème fraîche.

ORANGE AND GRAPEFRUIT SALAD

2 oranges; 2 ruby grapefruit;
1 avocado, peeled and stone removed;
400g large cooked prawns; 1 fennel bulb, finely sliced;
200g mixed salad leaves; 75ml orange juice;
200ml extra virgin olive oil; ½ tsp English mustard

1 Zest one orange. Cut the top and bottom off both oranges and the grapefruits. Slice off all the peel and pith from each and cut out all the individual segments. Hold over the bowl to catch the juice.

2 Slice the avocado and combine with the orange and grapefruit segments, prawns, fennel and salad leaves. Season. Mix the orange juice with the olive oil, mustard and zest. Season, dress the salad and serve.

64

COURGETTE AND MINT PASTA

500g tagliatelle; 3 courgettes, sliced;
2 garlic cloves, sliced; 1 red chilli, chopped;
400g raw prawns; 200ml crème fraîche;
A handful of mint, chopped; Juice of 1 lemon

1 Cook the pasta in boiling water until al dente, about 8–10 minutes. Drain, reserving 1 tbsp of the water.

2 Meanwhile, sweat the courgettes, garlic and chilli in oil until softened, about 5 minutes. Add the prawns and cook for a further 2 minutes until pink. Stir in the crème fraîche, mint, lemon juice and the spoonful of reserved pasta water.

3 Combine the sauce with the cooked pasta. Season. Serve.

PRAWNS

PILAF

2 red onions, chopped; 1 tsp garam masala;
4 cardamom pods, cracked; 200g basmati rice;
2 handfuls of peas; 500ml chicken or vegetable stock;
400g raw prawns; Juice and zest of 1 lemon;
A handful of coriander, chopped

1 Heat some olive oil in a pan and add the onions. Cook until soft, about 5 minutes. Add the garam masala and cardamom and cook for a further minute. Add the rice and peas and stir to coat in oil.

2 Add the stock and bring to the boil. Reduce the heat, cover and simmer for 10 minutes, adding the prawns 6 minutes in.

3 Remove from the heat. Add the lemon juice and zest and the coriander. Season. Fluff up with a fork. Serve.

TEMPURA

Vegetable oil, for deep-frying; 1 egg, beaten;
200ml sparkling water, chilled;
125g plain flour, extra for dusting;
400g raw prawns, tails on;
100g mayonnaise; 2 tsp wasabi paste

1 Heat a good amount of oil in a wok or deep frying pan. To check that the oil is hot enough, drop a square of bread into the oil – it should brown in 30 seconds. Place the egg and sparkling water in a bowl and stir. Add the flour, stir briefly but leave slightly lumpy.

2 Dust the prawns in the extra flour. Dip in the batter. Fry immediately, in batches, about 2 minutes until golden. Drain on some kitchen paper. Combine the mayonnaise and wasabi to create a dip and serve.

NOODLES

CHICKEN NOODLES

3 tbsp vegetable oil; 3 chicken breasts, cut into strips;
100g ginger, finely chopped; 3 garlic cloves, finely sliced;
200g spring onions, sliced; 600g straight-to-wok noodles;
200ml chicken stock; 100ml sherry;
3 tbsp soy sauce; 3 eggs, beaten

1 Heat the oil in a wok and when hot add the chicken followed by the ginger and garlic. Stir-fry for 2–3 minutes or until the chicken has coloured all over.

2 Add the onions and cook for another minute. Add the noodles and heat through, about 3–4 minutes.

3 Add the stock, sherry and soy and bring to the boil. Add the eggs and stir for 3 minutes or until the eggs are cooked. Serve.

PRAWN NOODLE SOUP

800ml chicken stock; 2 small red chillies, halved;
4cm knob of ginger, grated; 2 lemongrass stalks, bruised;
4 tbsp fish sauce; 4 tbsp lime juice;
1 tbsp sugar; 100g mushrooms, sliced;
150g rice noodles; 250g cooked prawns;
A handful of coriander, roughly chopped

1 Simmer the stock for 5 minutes with the chillies, ginger, lemongrass, fish sauce, lime juice and sugar. Strain and return the stock to the pan.

2 Add the mushrooms and noodles and cook for 5 minutes. Add the prawns and warm through for 1 minute. Serve with a sprinkling of the coriander.

MALAYSIAN CHICKEN NOODLES

600ml chicken stock
400ml coconut milk
1 tbsp Thai curry paste
3 chicken breasts, sliced
250g rice noodles
250g pre-cut mixed vegetable stir-fry
Juice of 1 lime

1 Bring the chicken stock, coconut milk and curry paste to the boil. Add the chicken and simmer for about 5 minutes or until the chicken is cooked.

2 Add the noodles and the stir-fry vegetable mix and warm through for 2–3 minutes. Squeeze over the lime juice and serve.

EGG NOODLE SALAD

400g egg noodles
2 tbsp rice vinegar
60ml soy sauce
2 tsp sesame oil
2cm knob of ginger, grated
1 large cucumber, cut into chunks
A handful of coriander, chopped
Grilled chicken or fish, to serve

1 Cook the egg noodles in boiling water, for about 8 minutes or until ready. Drain, rinse in cold water and leave to cool. Mix together the vinegar, soy sauce, sesame oil and ginger. Toss through the noodles.

2 Top with the chunks of cucumber and garnish with the coriander. Serve with grilled chicken or fish if desired.

FENNEL AND ORANGE

2 fennel bulbs

Zest and juice of 1 orange

125ml white wine

2 garlic cloves, crushed

1 tsp fennel seeds

4 small trout

A handful of coriander, chopped

1 Slice the fennel very thinly, ideally using a mandoline. Place in a roasting tray with a good glug of olive oil, orange zest and juice, wine, garlic and fennel seeds. Season well, toss to mix and cook at 180°C/Gas mark 4 for 15 minutes.

2 Place the trout on top, drizzle with some more oil, season and bake for a further 10–15 minutes or until cooked through. Sprinkle over the coriander and serve.

BAKED TROUT

TOMATO AND OLIVE

500g baby potatoes

8 tomatoes, halved

2 handfuls of green olives

A handful of basil, chopped

4 small trout

1 Place the potatoes in a roasting tray with a good glug of olive oil. Season and mix well to coat. Cook at 180°C/Gas mark 4 for 30–45 minutes until tender and golden.

2 Add the tomatoes, olives and basil to the tray and stir. Place the trout on top, drizzle with some more oil, season and bake for a further 10–15 minutes or until cooked through. Serve.

LEEKS

4 leeks
A handful of tarragon, chopped
125ml white wine
2 knobs of butter
4 small trout

1 Roughly slice the leeks. Place in a roasting tray with the tarragon and a good glug of olive oil. Season well and mix to coat in the oil. Add the wine and cook at 180°C/Gas mark 4 for 10 minutes.

2 Place dots of butter onto the leeks and lay the fish on top. Drizzle with some more oil, season and bake for a further 10–15 minutes or until cooked through. Serve.

ROSEMARY AND LEMON

4 small trout
A few sprigs of rosemary
2 garlic cloves, halved
1 lemon, sliced
125ml white wine

1 Stuff the trout with the rosemary, garlic and lemon slices. Place in a roasting tray. Drizzle with a good glug of olive oil and season well.

2 Add the wine and bake at 180°C/Gas mark 4 for 10–15 minutes or until cooked through. Serve.

SAFFRON

100g unsalted butter; 1 onion, finely chopped;
350g Arborio risotto rice; 125ml white wine;
A pinch of saffron strands;
1l hot chicken or vegetable stock;
50g Parmesan, freshly grated

1 Heat half the butter in a large pan and sweat the onion for 2–3 minutes or until soft. Add the rice and cook for 2 minutes, stirring continuously.

2 Add the wine and once it has evaporated add the saffron and hot stock, 2 ladles at a time, stirring continuously and waiting until it has all absorbed before adding more.

3 Once the rice is tender but still has a little bite (about 18 minutes), stir in the Parmesan and the remaining butter. Leave to stand, covered, for 5 minutes. Season, serve.

PEA, PRAWN AND MINT

3 tbsp olive oil; 1 onion, finely chopped;
350g Arborio risotto rice; 125ml white wine;
1l hot chicken or vegetable stock; 50g butter;
80g Parmesan, freshly grated; 300g cooked prawns;
250g peas, cooked; A handful of mint, finely chopped

1 Heat the oil in a large pan and sweat the onion for 2–3 minutes or until soft.

2 Add the rice and cook for 2 minutes, stirring continuously. Add the wine and once it has evaporated add the hot stock, 2 ladles at a time, stirring continuously and waiting until it has all absorbed before adding any more.

3 Once the rice is tender but still has a little bite (about 18 minutes), stir in the butter, Parmesan, prawns and peas. Leave to stand with a lid on for 5 minutes. Stir in the mint, season and serve.

MUSHROOM

50g dried porcini; 700ml hot chicken or vegetable stock;
1 onion, finely chopped; 250g mushrooms, sliced;
350g Arborio risotto rice; 125ml white wine;
80g Parmesan, grated; 50g butter; 30g parsley, chopped

1 Soak the porcini in 500ml of hot water for 20 minutes, strain. Add the liquid to the stock. Heat some oil in a large pan and sweat the onion for 2–3 minutes until soft. Add the mushrooms and cook for 5 minutes.

2 Add the rice and cook for another 2 minutes, stirring continuously. Add the wine and once evaporated add the hot stock, 2 ladles at a time, stirring continuously. Wait until it is absorbed before adding more.

3 Once the rice is tender but with some bite (about 18 minutes), stir in the Parmesan and butter and stand, covered, for 5 minutes. Stir in the parsley, season and serve.

BACON AND BROAD BEAN

300g broad beans; 8 rashers of smoked bacon, diced;
1 onion, finely chopped; 350g Arborio risotto rice;
125ml white wine; 1l hot chicken or vegetable stock;
80g Parmesan, grated; 50g butter

1 Cook the beans for 3 minutes in boiling water and drain. Heat some oil in a large pan and cook the bacon and onion for 2–3 minutes or until the onion is soft.

2 Add the rice and cook for 2 minutes, stirring continuously. Add the wine and once evaporated add the hot stock, 2 ladles at a time, stirring continuously and waiting until all of it is absorbed before adding more.

3 Once the rice is tender but with a bit of bite (about 18 minutes), stir in the Parmesan, butter and beans. Leave to stand with a lid on for 5 minutes, season and serve.

RISOTTO

SEA BASS

FENNEL AND ORANGE

A knob of butter
1 fennel bulb, very finely sliced
125ml white wine
Zest and juice of 2 oranges
4 sea bass fillets
A few basil leaves

1 Melt the butter in a frying pan, add the fennel and cook gently for 5–10 minutes or until soft. Add the wine, orange zest and juice and bubble to reduce.

2 In a separate pan, heat a dash of oil. Once hot, cook the fillets skin-side down for 3 minutes. Flip over and cook for a further minute. Season. Serve with the fennel, fennel juices and a few basil leaves.

LEMON AND CAPERS

Groundnut oil
4 sea bass fillets
A large knob of butter
Juice of 1 lemon
A handful of parsley, chopped
A handful of capers

1 Heat some groundnut oil in a pan. Once hot, cook the fillets skin-side down for 3 minutes. Flip over and cook for a further minute. Add the butter and lemon juice and as it melts spoon over the fish to baste. Add the parsley and capers. Season. Serve.

LETTUCE AND PEAS

100g smoked streaky bacon, sliced
60g unsalted butter
150g peas
200ml hot chicken stock
4 sea bass fillets
1 gem lettuce, shredded

1 Fry the bacon in a knob of butter until brown. Add the peas and stock. Cook for 5 minutes or until the peas are cooked.

2 Meanwhile, fry the fillets, skin-side down, in a glug of olive oil for 4–5 minutes. Flip over and cook for another minute.

3 Add the remaining butter and the lettuce to the pan of peas. Wilt the lettuce, season and serve with the fish placed on top of the bacon and peas.

CORIANDER AND VANILLA

125ml dry white wine; 1 tbsp white wine vinegar;
1 shallot, chopped; 3–4 coriander seeds, lightly crushed;
3–4 black peppercorns; 100g cold butter, cubed;
1 vanilla pod; 4 sea bass fillets

1 Boil the wine and the vinegar with the shallot, coriander seeds and peppercorns until reduced to a tbsp. Strain into a small bowl set over a pan of barely simmering water. Slowly add the butter, whisking continuously. Halve the vanilla pod lengthways, scrape out the seeds and whisk into the sauce. Keep warm.

2 Heat a dash of olive oil in a frying pan. Once hot, cook the fillets skin-side down for 3–4 minutes. Flip over and cook for a further minute. Serve with the sauce poured over the fish.

PESTO

2 garlic cloves
60g fresh basil, leaves only, extra for serving
25g pine nuts
1 tsp salt
150ml olive oil
50g Parmesan, freshly grated
500g tagliatelle

1 Pulse together the garlic, basil, pine nuts, salt and olive oil in a food processor until finely chopped. Stir in the Parmesan, adding more oil if necessary.

2 Cook the tagliatelle for 8–10 minutes in boiling salted water or until al dente. Drain and stir through the pesto. Serve with a few extra basil leaves.

PASTA SAUCE

CARBONARA

500g penne
200g smoked bacon, diced
1 tbsp olive oil
4 egg yolks
150ml double cream
100g Parmesan, freshly grated

1 Cook the penne in boiling salted water for 8–10 minutes or until al dente. Meanwhile, fry the bacon in the oil until crispy.

2 Whisk together the egg yolks, cream and Parmesan in a bowl. When the pasta is cooked, drain, reserving 2 tbsp of the cooking water. Place the pasta and reserved water into a bowl and add the egg mixture and the bacon. Combine well. Season with black pepper and serve.

GARLIC, CHILLI AND ANCHOVY

500g spaghetti

100ml olive oil

4 garlic cloves, lightly crushed

1 red chilli, chopped

6 anchovy fillets

1 Cook the pasta in boiling salted water, for about 8–10 minutes or until al dente.

2 Meanwhile, gently heat the oil in a pan. Add the crushed garlic, chilli and the anchovies and cook for 3–4 minutes or until the garlic has browned and the anchovies have melted.

3 Discard the garlic. Once cooked, drain the pasta, reserving a few tbsp of water. Place the pasta and reserved water in a bowl and mix in the sauce. Serve.

BOLOGNESE

1 tbsp olive oil; 4 rashers of bacon; 1 onion, chopped;
2 garlic cloves, crushed; 1 carrot, grated;
500g minced beef; 1 bay leaf; 125ml red wine;
400g tin of chopped tomatoes; 1 tbsp tomato purée;
1 tbsp Worcestershire sauce; 500g spaghetti;
A few basil leaves, chopped; Parmesan, freshly grated

1 Heat the oil in a pan and fry the bacon, onion, garlic and carrot for 3–4 minutes. Once soft, add the mince. Fry until brown, about 5 minutes. Add the bay leaf and wine and cook until the wine has evaporated.

2 Turn down the heat. Add the tomatoes, purée and Worcestershire sauce. Simmer, uncovered, for 1 hour or until thick and rich.

3 Meanwhile, cook the spaghetti in boiling salted water for 8–10 minutes or until al dente. Drain, stir in the sauce and serve with the basil and some Parmesan.

THYME BREADCRUMBS

2 tbsp plain flour; 2 eggs, beaten;
A handful of fine breadcrumbs;
A few sprigs of thyme; 4 cod fillets, skinned;
200g spinach; A knob of butter; 1 lemon

1 Place the flour, eggs and breadcrumbs into separate bowls. Season the flour well and mix the thyme leaves with the breadcrumbs. Dip each cod fillet in the flour, then the egg, then finally the breadcrumbs.

2 Heat some oil in a large pan. Add the cod. Cook, turning occasionally, until easily pierced by a sharp knife, about 6–8 minutes.

3 Meanwhile, wilt the spinach in a little boiling water for 2–3 minutes. Drain, squeezing out any excess water. Once the cod is cooked, add the butter and a squeeze of lemon juice and baste the fish. Serve the fish on top of a bed of spinach.

76

PROSCIUTTO AND SAGE

8 slices of prosciutto; 8 sage leaves;
4 cod fillets, skinned; A knob of butter;
Mixed salad, to serve

1 Lay 2 slices of prosciutto, so that they are slightly overlapping, on your work surface. Add 2 sage leaves to the middle of the slices. Place the cod fillet on top of the prosciutto slices and carefully wrap the cod until completely covered. Repeat with the remaining fillets.

2 Heat some olive oil in large pan. Add the cod and cook over a medium heat for about 5 minutes. Turn over and cook for another 5 minutes or until the fish is easily pierced with a knife. Add the butter and baste the fish. Season. Serve on top of a bed of salad.

MINTED PEAS

A knob of butter; 2 shallots or 1 onion, finely chopped;
300g frozen peas; 75ml crème fraîche;
A handful of mint, chopped; 4 cod fillets

1 Gently melt the butter in a small saucepan. Add the shallots and sauté until soft but not coloured, about 5 minutes. Meanwhile, cook the peas in boiling salted water for 5 minutes or until cooked. Drain.

2 Mix together the peas, shallots, crème fraîche, mint and seasoning. You can purée this sauce if you like. Keep warm until ready to serve.

3 Heat some oil in a large pan and add the fish, skin-side down. Cook for 4 minutes. Turn over and cook for another minute or so, or until it is easily pierced with a sharp knife. Serve, skin-side up, on the minted peas.

TOMATO, OLIVES AND BASIL

50ml olive oil, extra for frying
4 cod fillets
Juice of 1 lemon
8 cherry tomatoes, halved
A handful of pitted black olives, halved
A handful of basil, torn

1 Heat a little oil in a large pan and add the fish, skin-side down. Cook for 4 minutes. Turn over and cook for another minute or so, or until it is easily pierced with a sharp knife.

2 Meanwhile, place the 50ml of olive oil and the lemon juice in a small saucepan. Add the tomatoes, olives and basil. Warm gently but do not let boil.

3 Serve the cod, skin-side up, on top of the tomato sauce.

COD

PORK CHOPS

FENNEL, CHILLI AND TOMATO

4 large pork chops; 4 garlic cloves, crushed;
A pinch of chilli flakes; 2 tsp fennel seeds;
400g tin of chopped tomatoes;
8 small potatoes, peeled; A knob of butter

1 Heat some oil in an ovenproof pan and fry the chops for a minute on each side, plus a minute on the fatty edge to seal. Add the garlic, chilli and fennel seeds and cook for a further 2 minutes. Add the tomatoes.

2 Transfer the pan to the oven and bake at 200°C/Gas mark 6 for 10–15 minutes or until the sauce is thick and the meat is cooked through.

3 Meanwhile, bring the potatoes to the boil for 15 minutes in salted water or until easily pierced with a knife. Drain, mash and add some butter. Season the chops and serve with the mash.

PAPRIKA SPICED

2 red onions, finely sliced; 4 large pork chops;
2 garlic cloves, crushed; 1 tbsp mild smoked paprika;
½ lemon, sliced; 200ml chicken stock;
Couscous, grilled red peppers and olives, to serve

1 Combine the onions, chops, garlic, paprika and lemon. Season well and leave to marinate for at least 30 minutes.

2 Place the chops in a hot ovenproof pan and cook for a minute on each side, plus a minute on the fatty edge to seal. Add the marinade and stock, bring to boil and transfer to a 200°C/Gas mark 6 oven.

3 Cook for 10–15 minutes until cooked through. Allow to rest for 5 minutes. Serve with some couscous, grilled peppers and olives, with the pan juices poured over.

LEMON

4 large pork chops; 2 courgettes, roughly chopped;
A large handful of cherry tomatoes, halved;
A handful of basil leaves, torn;
Juice of 1 lemon; A knob of butter

1 Heat a drizzle of olive oil in a large ovenproof pan. Season the chops and fry for 1 minute on each side, plus 1 minute on the fatty edge to seal.

2 Drizzle the courgettes, tomatoes and basil with a little oil and roast in the oven at 200°C/Gas mark 6 for 15 minutes. Add the chops, pour over the lemon juice and return to the oven for 10 minutes.

3 Remove the tray from the oven, add the butter and leave to melt. Leave to rest for 5 minutes in the pan, basting occasionally.

PEARS

4 large pork chops; A handful of rosemary, chopped;
4 garlic cloves, crushed; Juice of 1 lemon;
4 tbsp olive oil; 2 pears, cored, peeled and quartered;
A knob of butter

1 Put the chops in a strong food bag and add the rosemary, garlic, lemon juice, oil and seasoning. Seal the bag, massage to mix together, and leave to marinate for a minimum of 30 minutes.

2 Place the chops in a hot pan and cook for 3–4 minutes on each side. Add the pears and a knob of butter and cook for 3–4 minutes or until the pears are slightly caramelised. Remove the pan from the heat and allow to rest for 3–4 minutes, basting occasionally with the butter and juices.

SWEETCORN FRITTERS

150g plain flour
1 tsp baking powder
150ml milk
50g butter, melted
340g tin of sweetcorn
Grilled bacon, grilled tomatoes and scrambled egg,
to serve

1 Mix the flour, baking powder, milk and butter until it is a smooth batter. Add the drained sweetcorn.

2 Heat a splash of oil in a pan. Add small dollops of the sweetcorn batter and cook for 1–2 minutes on each side. Serve with strips of grilled bacon, some scrambled egg and a few grilled tomatoes.

SWEETCORN

CHOWDER

A knob of butter; 1 onion, chopped;
1 leek, chopped; 2 potatoes, diced;
800ml hot chicken or vegetable stock;
200ml double cream; 2 x 340g tins of sweetcorn;
Juice of ½ a lemon; 70g pork scratchings, crumbled;
A small handful of parsley, chopped

1 Melt the butter in a saucepan. Gently sweat the onion, leek and potatoes for 10 minutes.

2 Add the stock, cream and the drained sweetcorn. Cook for 3–4 minutes or until the potatoes feel soft and are easily pierced with a knife. Season.

3 Stir through the lemon juice and scatter with crumbled pork scratchings and some chopped parsley.

RISOTTO CAKE

1 onion, chopped; 1 garlic clove, chopped;
1 tsp curry powder; 200g basmati rice, well rinsed;
1 vegetable stock cube; A knob of butter;
2 handfuls of fine breadcrumbs; 2 eggs, separated;
150ml double cream; 340g tin of sweetcorn;
50g Parmesan, grated; A handful of parsley, chopped

1 Sweat the onion and garlic in oil for 5–8 minutes. Add the curry powder and cook for a minute. Add the rice and stir to coat. Add 500ml boiling water and a crumbled stock cube. Cover. Simmer for 10 minutes or until the liquid is absorbed. Fluff with a fork.

2 Grease a 20cm cake tin with butter and dust with breadcrumbs. Mix the egg yolks with the rice, cream, sweetcorn, Parmesan, parsley and seasoning. Whisk the egg whites to soft peaks. Fold into the rice and spoon into the cake tin. Bake at 180°C/Gas mark 4 for 20 minutes. Cool and serve sliced.

SALAD

400g tin of kidney beans
1 red onion, chopped
2 avocados, diced
340g tin of sweetcorn
8 cherry tomatoes, quartered
1 red chilli, finely chopped
Juice of 1 lime
200g feta
A small handful of coriander, chopped

1 Drain the kidney beans and mix with the onion, avocado, drained sweetcorn, tomatoes and chilli. Squeeze over the lime juice and drizzle with some olive oil. Season (using not too much salt) and stir.

2 Crumble over the feta and scatter with the coriander. Serve.

TUNA AND SWEETCORN SALAD

185g tin of tuna
200g tin of sweetcorn
400g tin of cannellini or black-eyed beans
A small handful of capers
2 baby gem lettuces
3 tbsp natural yoghurt
1 tbsp crème fraîche
Juice and zest of ½ a lemon
A handful of parsley, chopped

1 Drain the tuna, sweetcorn and beans. Mix with the capers. Place the lettuce leaves in a bowl and top with the tuna mixture.

2 Combine the yoghurt, crème fraîche and lemon juice and zest, adding lots of salt. Drizzle over the lettuce leaves, scatter with parsley and serve.

NIÇOISE

6 baby potatoes; A large handful of French beans;
4 eggs; 2 tbsp red wine vinegar; 1 tsp Dijon mustard;
100ml extra virgin olive oil; 2 garlic cloves, crushed;
2 baby gem lettuces; 185g tin of tuna;
4 tomatoes, quartered; 8 anchovy fillets;
A handful of black olives, halved

1 In separate pans, cook the potatoes and beans in salted water until cooked. The potatoes will take about 10 minutes, the beans 6 minutes. Refresh both in cold water. Soft-boil the eggs – about 5 minutes – then refresh in cold water and peel. Halve the potatoes and beans and quarter the eggs.

2 Mix the vinegar, mustard, oil and garlic to form a vinaigrette. Arrange the lettuce leaves in a bowl, top with all the ingredients and drizzle over the dressing. Season, serve.

TUNA PASTA

1 onion, chopped; 2 garlic cloves;
A pinch of chilli flakes; 2 tomatoes, finely chopped;
Juice and zest of ½ a lemon; 2 x 185g tins of tuna;
125ml white wine; 375g fusilli pasta;
2 handfuls of rocket; Parmesan, freshly grated

1 Heat a drizzle of oil in a large pan and cook the onion, garlic and chilli over a low heat until soft, about 4 minutes. Add the tomatoes, lemon juice and zest and the drained tuna.

2 Add the wine and reduce the heat. Season and gently cook for about 10 minutes, stirring occasionally.

3 Meanwhile, cook the pasta in salted boiling water for about 8–10 minutes or until al dente. Drain and add to the pan of tuna sauce. Stir through the rocket and allow to wilt. Serve with some Parmesan.

OLIVE AND TOMATO PASTA

1 onion, chopped; 2 garlic cloves, crushed;
A small handful of capers; A handful of black olives;
400g tin of chopped tomatoes; 2 x 185g tins of tuna;
375g penne pasta; Juice of ½ a lemon;
A handful of parsley, chopped; Parmesan, freshly grated

1 Heat a drizzle of oil in a large pan and cook the onion and garlic over a low heat until soft, about 4 minutes. Add the capers, olives and tomatoes.

2 Cook until reduced, about 10 minutes, stirring occasionally. Add the drained tuna for the last minute to warm through.

3 Meanwhile, cook the pasta in salted boiling water for about 8–10 minutes or until al dente. Drain and add to the pan of tuna sauce. Season with lemon juice. Serve with a sprinkling of parsley and Parmesan.

TINNED TUNA

GINGER AND SOY

2 tbsp honey; 2cm knob of ginger, grated;
1 garlic clove; 2 tsp five spice;
1 tbsp soy sauce; 2 tbsp sesame or olive oil;
8 chicken thighs; Cooked rice, to serve

1 Mix the honey, ginger, garlic, five spice, soy sauce and oil. Pour over the chicken thighs and marinate for at least 1 hour, but preferably overnight.

2 Remove the thighs from the marinade and place in a ovenproof dish. Roast at 200°C/ Gas mark 6 for 15 minutes, turn, brush with more marinade and cook for a further 10–15 minutes or until well browned and when pierced with a knife the juices run clear. Serve with some rice.

CHICKEN THIGHS

LEMON AND GARLIC

3 tbsp olive oil

2 sprigs of rosemary, chopped

2 garlic cloves, crushed

2 lemons

8 chicken thighs

1 Mix the oil, rosemary and garlic with the juice of 1 lemon. Season well. Pour over the chicken thighs and marinate for at least 1 hour, but preferably overnight.

2 Remove the thighs from the marinade and place in an ovenproof dish. Add some slices of lemon to the pan and roast at 200°C/Gas mark 6 for 15 minutes. Then turn the chicken, brush with more marinade and cook for a further 10–15 minutes or until well browned and when pierced the juices run clear. Serve.

HONEY AND MUSTARD

2 tbsp olive oil
2 tbsp grain mustard
1 tbsp honey
8 chicken thighs
Cooked French beans and cherry tomatoes, to serve

1 Mix together the oil, mustard and honey and brush over the chicken thighs. Season.

2 Roast at 200°C/Gas mark 6 for 15 minutes, then turn the thighs, brush with some more marinade and return to the oven for a further 10–15 minutes or until well browned and when pierced with a knife the juices run clear. Serve with some French beans and cherry tomatoes.

SESAME AND CHILLI

3 tbsp olive oil; Juice of ½ a lemon; 1 tbsp honey;
1 tbsp sumac; 2 sprigs of thyme, chopped;
A pinch of chilli flakes; 8 chicken thighs;
1 tsp sesame seeds; Couscous, to serve

1 Mix together the oil, lemon, honey, sumac, thyme and chilli. Season well. Pour over the chicken thighs and marinate for at least 1 hour, but preferably overnight.

2 Remove the thighs from the marinade and place in an ovenproof dish. Roast at 200°C/Gas mark 6 for 15 minutes, turn, brush with more marinade and sprinkle over the sesame seeds. Cook for a further 10–15 minutes or until well browned and when pierced with a knife the juices run clear. Serve with couscous flavoured with lemon and parsley.

ROAST BEEF

TRADITIONAL

1kg sirloin
1 tsp caraway seeds, crushed (optional)
1 tsp mustard seeds, crushed (optional)
Watercress, to serve

1 Rub the meat with olive oil. Season very well and sprinkle with the crushed caraway and mustard seeds, if using.

2 Place in a roasting tin and cook for 15 minutes at 230°C/Gas mark 8. As soon as the 15 minutes are up, turn the oven down to 180°C/Gas mark 4 and cook for 25–30 minutes if you want it rare; 35–40 minutes if you want it medium. Let rest in the pan for 15 minutes once out of the oven. Carve and serve on a bed of watercress.

SALSA VERDE

1kg sirloin; A large knob of butter; 8 anchovy fillets;
1 tbsp vinegar; 6 tbsp olive oil; A small handful of capers;
1 tsp French mustard; A handful of parsley;
A handful of basil; 2 garlic cloves

1 Cut slashes over the top of the beef. Mash the butter and anchovies together and rub over the meat. Season.

2 Place in a roasting tin and cook for 15 minutes at 230°C/Gas mark 8. As soon as the 15 minutes are up, turn the oven down to 180°C/Gas mark 4 and cook for 25–30 minutes if you want it rare; 35–40 minutes if you want it medium. Let rest in the pan for 15 minutes once out of the oven and baste.

3 Combine the remaining ingredients in a food processer and briefly pulse to form a coarse sauce. Serve drizzled over the beef.

MUSTARD

1 large onion, diced; 2 bay leaves; A knob of butter;
150g fresh breadcrumbs; 100g wholegrain mustard;
1kg sirloin

1 Gently fry the onion and bay leaves in the butter until soft, about 10 minutes. Discard the leaves and mix the onions with the breadcrumbs, mustard and enough olive oil to bind the mixture together. Mix well to form a coarse paste and spread over the top of the sirloin.

2 Place in a roasting tin and cook for 15 minutes at 230°C/Gas mark 8. As soon as the 15 minutes are up, turn the oven down to 180°C/Gas mark 4 and cook for 25–30 minutes if you want it rare; 35–40 minutes if you want it medium. Let rest in the pan for 15 minutes once out of the oven. Serve.

POT ROAST

1kg topside or silverside; 2 red onions, sliced;
4 garlic cloves, unpeeled; 1 celery stick, sliced;
4 tomatoes; 4 carrots; A bunch of thyme; 2 bay leaves;
125ml red or white wine; 150ml chicken or beef stock

1 Add some olive oil to a large ovenproof pan over a high heat. Add the meat and cook until browned on all sides, about 10 minutes. Remove the meat and add the onions and garlic to the pan. Reduce the heat and cook until browned, about 10 minutes.

2 Season, return the meat to the pan and add all the remaining vegetables, herbs, wine and stock. Bring to a simmer, cover with a lid and cook at 150°C/Gas mark 2 for 2 hours or until tender. Remove the meat and the vegetables from the pan and serve together on a platter.

CHERRY SAUCE

4 duck breasts; 125ml red wine; 2 garlic cloves, crushed;
A sprig of thyme; 300ml chicken stock;
200g cherries, pitted and halved; A large knob of butter

1 Score the skin of the duck breasts and season. Place skin-side down in a cold pan. Cook for 8 minutes on a low–medium heat or until the skin is crisp. Drain any fat from the pan, turn the meat and fry for a further minute to colour. Transfer to a 190°C/Gas mark 5 oven for 4–6 minutes. Remove from the oven and rest on a board for 5 minutes.

2 Place the wine, garlic and thyme in the empty duck pan. Boil for 5 minutes or until reduced. Add the stock and boil for a further 5 minutes or until reduced. Stir in the cherries and cook for another 5 minutes. Whisk in the butter. Slice the duck breast and serve with the sauce.

HONEY, STAR ANISE AND GINGER

4 duck breasts; 1 tsp five spice; 200ml chicken stock;
3 tbsp honey; 3 tbsp soy sauce; 2cm of ginger, grated;
3 star anise; A pinch of chilli flakes; Juice of 1 lime;
Cooked ribbon carrots and courgettes, to serve

1 Score the skin of the duck breasts and season with five spice. Place skin-side down in a cold pan. Cook for 8 minutes on a low–medium heat or until the skin is crisp. Drain any fat from the pan, turn the meat and fry for a further minute to colour. Transfer to a 190°C/Gas mark 5 oven for 4–6 minutes. Remove from the oven and let rest on a board for 5 minutes.

2 Place the remaining ingredients in the empty duck pan. Boil until reduced by half, about 5 minutes. Strain. Slice the duck breast and serve with the sauce and some cooked carrots and courgettes.

MADEIRA SAUCE

4 duck breasts; 1 onion, sliced; 1 bay leaf;
A sprig of thyme; 1 garlic clove, crushed; 100ml red wine;
1 tbsp sherry vinegar; 200ml Madeira;
400ml chicken stock; A knob of butter;
Cooked peas, broad beans and cabbage, to serve

1 Cook the duck breasts in the same way as step 1 of the Cherry Sauce recipe above.

2 Sweat the onion, bay, thyme and garlic in the empty duck pan until soft, about 10 minutes. Season, add the wine and vinegar, and cook until evaporated, about 5 minutes. Add the Madeira and boil until reduced by half, about 5 minutes. Add the stock and again boil until reduced by half, about 8 minutes. Whisk in the butter and strain. Slice the duck. Serve with the sauce and some cooked peas, broad beans and cabbage.

ORANGE SAUCE

4 duck breasts
4 shallots, sliced
1 tbsp sherry vinegar
125ml white wine
Juice and zest of 2 oranges
1 tbsp brown sugar
Cooked French beans, to serve

1 Cook the duck breasts in the same way as step 1 of the Cherry Sauce recipe above.

2 Sweat the shallots in some olive oil in the empty duck pan until soft, about 8 minutes. Add the vinegar and white wine and boil until almost completely evaporated, about 5 minutes.

3 Add the juice and zest of both oranges and the sugar. Boil until thickened, about 10 minutes. Slice the duck. Serve with the sauce and some cooked green beans.

DUCK BREASTS

FRENCH

1.8kg mussels; A knob of unsalted butter;
1 garlic clove, finely chopped; 1 onion, finely chopped;
125ml dry white wine; 4 tbsp double cream;
3 tbsp chopped fresh parsley; French bread, to serve

1 Thoroughly wash and clean the mussels. Discard any that do not close tight when tapped, or feel too heavy (these will be full of grit). Melt the butter in a large saucepan over a high heat. Add the garlic and onion and cook for 1 minute.

2 Add the wine. Bring to the boil and add the mussels. Cook with the lid on for 3–4 minutes or until most of the mussels have opened. Discard any that have not opened.

3 Add the cream and stir well. Season with pepper only. Serve sprinkled with the parsley and some chunks of bread.

90

MUSSELS

THAI

1.8kg mussels; 2 tbsp vegetable oil; 1 onion, chopped;
3 garlic cloves, crushed; 2 lemongrass stalks, chopped;
2cm knob of ginger, finely chopped;
1 red chilli, chopped; 250ml white wine;
3 tbsp fish sauce; A handful of coriander, chopped;
Juice of 1 lime; Cooked rice and lime wedges, to serve

1 Thoroughly wash the mussels. Discard any that do not close when tapped, or feel too heavy. Heat the oil in a large saucepan and gently cook the onion, garlic, lemongrass, ginger and chilli for 5 minutes.

2 Add the wine and fish sauce. Bring to the boil and add the mussels. Cook with the lid on for 3–4 minutes or until the mussels are open. Discard any that have not opened.

3 Add the coriander and lime juice. Only season with pepper and serve with rice.

BRITISH

1.8kg mussels; A knob of butter;
1 celery stick, finely sliced; 1 carrot, finely chopped;
2 garlic cloves, chopped; 250ml dry cider;
150ml crème fraîche; 1 tbsp chopped tarragon;
1 tbsp chopped chives; French bread, to serve

1 Thoroughly wash and clean the mussels. Discard any that do not close when tapped, or feel too heavy. Melt the butter in a large saucepan over a high heat. Add the celery, carrot and garlic and cook for 2 minutes.

2 Add the cider. Bring to the boil and add the mussels. Cook with the lid on for 3–4 minutes or until most of the mussels are open. Discard any that have not opened.

3 Stir in the crème fraîche and herbs. Only season with pepper and serve with bread.

INDIAN

1.8kg mussels; 2 tbsp vegetable oil; 1 large onion, sliced;
2cm knob of ginger, finely chopped; 2 tsp curry powder;
250ml fish stock; 200ml coconut milk;
A small handful of coriander, chopped

1 Thoroughly wash and clean the mussels. Discard any that do not close when tapped, or feel too heavy. Heat the oil in a large frying pan, add the onion and ginger and cook until the onion is soft, about 5 minutes. Add the curry powder and cook for a further minute, stirring often.

2 Add the stock. Bring to the boil and add the mussels. Cook with the lid on for 3–4 minutes or until the mussels are open. Discard any mussels that have not opened.

3 Add the coconut milk and coriander, boil for a minute or so to reduce and make the sauce green. Season with pepper only.

PAPILLOTE

CHICKEN WITH COURGETTE AND MINT

4 small skinless chicken breasts;
2 carrots, cut into matchsticks;
2 courgettes, cut into matchsticks;
2 tbsp olive oil; 400g tin of cannellini beans, drained;
A large handful of mint, chopped;
2 tbsp lemon juice; 125ml white wine

1 Cut four 30x30cm squares of strong foil. Fold each in half and seal the 2 shorter sides of the foil by folding tightly. This should form a pocket with a long opening in the top.

2 Share all the ingredients equally between the 4 parcels. Season. Seal well by folding over the open top edge twice.

3 Cook at 220°C/Gas mark 7 for about 30 minutes or until the chicken is white and completely cooked. Carefully open and serve.

CHICKEN WITH MUSHROOMS

4 small skinless chicken breasts;
4 handfuls of mushrooms, sliced;
4 garlic cloves, sliced; 250ml white wine;
200ml double cream; 4 large knobs of butter;
A handful of tarragon, chopped

1 Cut four 30x30cm squares of strong foil. Fold each in half and seal the 2 shorter sides of the foil by folding tightly. This should form a pocket with a long opening in the top.

2 Share all the ingredients equally between the 4 parcels. Season. Seal well by folding over the open top edge twice.

3 Cook at 220°C/Gas mark 7 for about 30 minutes or until the chicken is white and completely cooked. Carefully open and serve.

COD AND CHORIZO

4 small cod fillets; 150g chorizo sausage, sliced;
200g cherry tomatoes, halved;
2 tbsp olive oil; 3 tbsp white wine;
1 tbsp sherry vinegar; A handful of parsley, chopped

1 Cut four 30x30cm squares of strong foil. Fold each in half and seal the 2 shorter sides of the foil by folding tightly. This should form a pocket with a long opening in the top.

2 Share all the ingredients equally between the 4 parcels. Season. Seal well by folding over the open top edge twice.

3 Cook at 190°C/Gas mark 5 for about 15 minutes or until the fish feels firm to the touch and is completely cooked. Carefully open and serve.

SEA BASS WITH FENNEL AND BASIL

4 sea bass fillets; 2 fennel bulbs, finely sliced;
A handful of basil leaves, chopped;
125ml white wine; 15ml Pernod (optional);
4 small knobs of butter

1 Cut four 30x30cm squares of strong foil. Fold each in half and seal the 2 shorter sides of the foil by folding tightly. This should form a pocket with a long opening in the top.

2 Share all the ingredients equally between the 4 parcels. Season. Seal well by folding over the open top edge twice.

3 Cook at 190°C/Gas mark 5 for about 15 minutes or until the fish feels firm to the touch and is completely cooked. Carefully open and serve.

CLASSIC

5kg whole goose; 1 lemon, halved; 2 tbsp honey

1 Prick the goose skin with a fork. Rub with the lemon halves and season well, inside and out. Place the lemon halves into the cavity and place the goose on a rack over a roasting tin.

2 Cook for 30 minutes at 200°C/Gas mark 6. Pour off the fat from the pan (keep for when you are making roast potatoes) and turn the heat down to 180°C/Gas mark 4. Cook for a further 3 hours, basting occasionally. Cover with some foil if it starts to turn too brown.

3 Ten minutes before it is cooked, brush the skin with the honey and return to the oven. Once done, the juices should run clear when the thickest part is pierced with a knife. Rest for 20 minutes before serving.

MARMALADE

5kg whole goose; 1 orange; A few sprigs of thyme; 3 bay leaves; 4 tbsp marmalade

1 Prick the goose skin with a fork. Season well, inside and out. Pierce the orange several times with a knife and place the orange and herbs into the goose cavity. Place on a rack over a roasting tin.

2 Cook for 30 minutes at 200°C/Gas mark 6. Pour off the fat (keep for roast potatoes) and turn the heat down to 180°C/Gas mark 4. Cook for a further 2½ hours, basting occasionally. Cover with some foil if it starts to turn too brown.

3 Heat the marmalade in a saucepan. Brush over the goose breast and return to the oven for a further 30 minutes, uncovered. Check the juices run clear when the goose is pierced. Rest for 20 minutes before serving.

HERBY

5kg whole goose;
2 sprigs each of sage, rosemary and thyme;
1 garlic bulb head; 1 red onion, roughly chopped

1 Prick the goose skin with a fork. Season well, inside and out. Place the herbs, garlic and onion in the goose cavity. Place on a rack over a roasting tin.

2 Cook for 30 minutes at 200°C/Gas mark 6. Pour off the fat from the pan (keep for roast potatoes) and turn the heat down to 180°C/Gas mark 4. Cook for a further 3 hours, basting occasionally. Cover with some foil if it starts to turn too brown.

3 Once done, the juices should run clear when the thickest part is pierced with a knife. Rest for 20 minutes before serving.

SPICED

3 lemons; 3 limes; 3 tbsp honey;
2 tsp Chinese five spice; 5kg whole goose;
2 sprigs each of rosemary and thyme

1 Add the juice and zest of the citrus fruits to a pan with the honey and five spice. Bring to the boil. Prick the goose skin with a fork. Stuff the cavity with the squeezed fruits and the herbs. Glaze the top with the lemon mixture. Place on a rack over a roasting tin.

2 Cook for 30 minutes at 200°C/Gas mark 6. Pour off the fat (keep for roast potatoes) and turn the heat down to 180°C/Gas mark 4. Cook for 3 hours, basting occasionally. Cover with foil if it starts to turn too brown.

3 Once done, the juices should run clear when pierced with a knife. Rest for 20 minutes before serving.

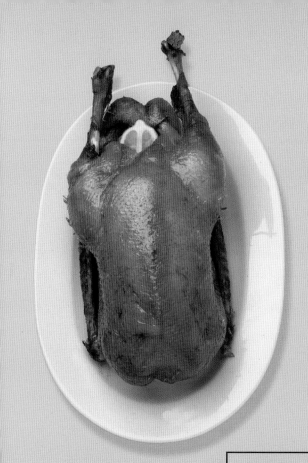

ROAST GOOSE

PILAU RICE

A large knob of butter;
2 small onions, roughly chopped;
1 tbsp curry powder; 1 cup of basmati rice;
2 cups of hot vegetable stock; 1 cinnamon stick;
2 star anise; 6 cardamom pods;
6 cloves; A handful of peas

1 Melt half the butter in a saucepan, add the onions and cook for about 10 minutes or until soft. Add the curry powder and cook for a further 2 minutes, stirring occasionally.

2 Add the rice, stock, cinnamon stick, star anise, cardamom, cloves and peas. Simmer with a lid on until the rice is cooked and all the stock has been absorbed, about 10 minutes.

3 Add the remaining butter and seasoning, fluff up with a fork and serve with your favourite curry.

KEDGEREE

A large knob of butter; 2 small onions, roughly chopped;
1 tbsp curry powder; 1 cup of basmati rice;
2 cups of hot vegetable stock; 1 cinnamon stick;
2 star anise; A handful of peas; 4 pre-cooked trout fillets;
Juice of 1 lemon; A small handful of parsley, chopped

1 Melt half the butter in a saucepan, add the onions and cook for about 10 minutes or until soft. Add the curry powder and cook for a further 2 minutes, stirring occasionally.

2 Add the rice, stock, cinnamon stick, star anise and peas. Simmer with a lid on until the rice is cooked and all the liquid is absorbed, about 10 minutes.

3 Break up the trout. Add the remaining butter, trout, lemon juice, parsley and seasoning to the rice. Fluff up with a fork and serve as is.

PERSIAN

A large knob of butter; 1 large onion, roughly chopped;
½ tsp all spice; ½ tsp cinnamon; 1 cup of basmati rice;
2 cups of hot vegetable stock; ½ tsp saffron strands;
A handful of dried apricots; A handful of dried cherries;
A small handful of coriander, chopped;
A handful of toasted pistachios, to serve

1 Melt half the butter in a saucepan. Add the onion and cook, with the lid on, for about 15 minutes until golden. Add the all spice and cinnamon and cook for another minute.

2 Add the rice, stock, saffron, apricots and cherries. Simmer with the lid on until the rice is cooked and the liquid is all absorbed, about 10 minutes.

3 Add the remaining butter and seasoning. Fluff up with a fork and serve scattered with the coriander and pistachios.

EGG FRIED RICE

2 tbsp vegetable oil
600g cooked short-grain rice
A handful of cooked peas
A handful of beansprouts
2–3 spring onions, sliced
3 eggs, beaten
1 tsp sesame oil
1 tsp soy sauce

1 Heat the oil in a wok. Add the pre-cooked rice and stir-fry for 3 minutes. Add the peas, beansprouts and spring onions and stir-fry for a further minute to warm through.

2 Add the eggs and stir well to coat all of the rice. Stir-fry until the egg is cooked, about 3–4 minutes. Drizzle over the sesame oil and soy sauce to season and serve.

SAUSAGES

CASSEROLE

1 tbsp olive oil; 6 sausages, chopped;
2 onions, chopped; 1 leek, sliced;
2 celery sticks, sliced; 4 potatoes, chopped;
A few sprigs of thyme; 2 bay leaves;
250ml dry cider; 1 tbsp chopped parsley

1 Heat the oil in a pan. Add the sausages and brown over a medium heat for 3–4 minutes. Remove the sausages from the pan and add the onions, leek and celery. Cook until soft, about 10 minutes.

2 Return the sausages to the pan along with the potatoes, thyme and bay leaves. Add enough cider to cover. Season and bring to a gentle simmer. Cook, covered, for 1 hour.

3 Scatter over the parsley and serve.

FENNEL PASTA

8 large sausages; 1 fennel bulb, sliced;
2 tsp fennel seeds, crushed; ½ tsp crushed dried chillies;
250ml white wine; 500g penne pasta; A knob of butter;
A handful of grated Parmesan;
A handful of parsley, chopped

1 Heat a splash of olive oil in a large frying pan. Cut open the sausages and crumble the meat into the pan. Add the sliced fennel, seeds and chillies and cook, stirring occasionally, until the meat and fennel are caramelised, about 10 minutes. Add the wine and allow to bubble and reduce by half.

2 Meanwhile, cook the pasta in boiling salted water for 8–10 minutes or until al dente. Drain, adding a couple of spoonfuls of the cooking water to the meat. Combine the pasta with the sausage and stir in the butter, seasoning, Parmesan and the parsley. Serve.

TOAD IN THE HOLE

8 large sausages; 1 tbsp olive oil;
100g plain flour; 3 eggs;
200ml milk; Onion gravy, to serve

1 Place the sausages and the oil in a metal roasting tin and cook in the oven at 220°C/Gas mark 7 for about 10 minutes or until the sausages have browned.

2 Meanwhile, sift the flour into a mixing bowl. Crack in the eggs and gradually whisk in the milk to make a smooth batter. Season well.

3 Pour the batter over the sausages and into the roasting tin. Return to the oven and cook for 20–30 minutes or until the batter is puffed up, golden and crisp on top. Serve with a drizzle of onion gravy if you like.

LENTILS AND SPINACH

8 sausages; 2 onions, sliced;
2 tsp curry powder; 250g puy lentils;
1 chicken stock cube; 240g baby spinach;
Juice of 1 lemon; A handful of parsley and mint, chopped;
200g natural yoghurt

1 Cook the sausages at 180°C/Gas mark 4 for about 20 minutes.

2 Meanwhile, fry the onion in olive oil for about 10 minutes until soft. Add the curry powder, cook for another minute. Add the lentils, crumbled stock cube and enough water to cover. Cook for about 15 minutes or until soft. Drain.

3 Add the spinach and allow to wilt. Season and add the lemon juice. Stir through the yoghurt and herbs. Serve with the sausages.

CHICKPEA AND TOMATO BAKE

2 garlic cloves, sliced; 2 onions, sliced;
2 courgettes, sliced; 2 x 400g tins of chopped tomatoes;
A pinch of fine sugar; 400g tin of chickpeas, drained;
A handful of basil, torn; 2 handfuls of breadcrumbs;
A handful of grated Parmesan; Zest of 1 lemon

1 In a large saucepan, gently sweat the garlic, onions and courgettes in a little olive oil until soft, about 10 minutes. Season. Stir in the tomatoes and sugar and let simmer for about 20 minutes, uncovered.

2 Stir in the chickpeas and the basil and pour the mixture into a baking dish. Spread even. Combine the breadcrumbs, Parmesan and lemon zest and sprinkle over the top of the tomato mixture. Bake at 180°C/Gas mark 4 for about 20 minutes or until golden.

CHICKPEAS

CHICKPEA AND FETA

2 red onions, sliced
A pinch of chilli flakes
2 tsp paprika
Juice and zest of 2 lemons
2 x 400g tins of chickpeas
200g feta, crumbled
A large handful of parsley, chopped

1 In a saucepan, gently sweat the onions in olive oil until soft, about 10 minutes. Stir in the chilli and paprika and cook for 1 minute.

2 Add the lemon juice and zest, chickpeas and some of their water. Turn up the heat and cook, stirring, until warmed through, about 5 minutes. Stir in half the feta.

3 Transfer to a serving dish. Sprinkle over the remaining feta, the parsley and add some seasoning. Serve.

CHICKPEA AND CHORIZO CASSEROLE

2 red onions, sliced
200g chorizo sausage, diced
1l hot chicken stock
½ Savoy cabbage, shredded
2 x 400g tins of chickpeas, drained
1 lemon

1 Heat a dash of olive oil in a large saucepan. Add the onions and chorizo. Cook gently until soft, about 10 minutes. Season well.

2 Stir in the stock and bring to the boil. Add the cabbage and the chickpeas and simmer for 4–5 minutes or until the cabbage is just cooked and slightly wilted.

3 Serve with a squeeze of lemon juice and a drizzle of olive oil.

CHICKPEA FRITTERS

125g plain flour; ½ tsp baking powder;
2 eggs, separated; 2 tbsp milk;
2 tbsp tahini; 400g tin of chickpeas, drained;
A handful of coriander, chopped;
1 chilli, finely chopped; Tzatziki, to serve

1 Stir the flour and baking powder in a mixing bowl. Add the egg yolks, milk and tahini and whisk to form a light batter. Add the chickpeas, crushing slightly with a fork to break up. Season.

2 In a separate bowl, whisk the egg whites to form soft peaks. Gently fold the egg whites, coriander and chilli into the batter using a metal spoon.

3 Heat a dash of oil in a frying pan. Add small spoonfuls of batter and cook for 2 minutes on each side. Serve with tzatziki.

LAMB AND MINT

600g lamb neck, minced; 2 onions, sliced;
2 carrots, chopped; 2 garlic cloves, chopped;
1 tbsp flour; 125ml red wine; 300ml hot chicken stock;
1 tbsp tomato purée; 1 tbsp Worcestershire sauce;
A handful of dried mint; 1kg potatoes; 100g butter

1 Heat 1 tbsp olive oil in a pan. Cook the lamb until well coloured and remove with a slotted spoon. Cook the onions, carrots and garlic for 10 minutes until soft. Return the lamb to the pan, season, add flour and stir. Add the wine and leave to reduce by half.

2 Add the stock, purée, Worcestershire sauce and mint. Simmer for 30 minutes. Meanwhile, put the potatoes on to boil. Once cooked – about 15 minutes – mash with the butter. Transfer the meat to a pie dish and cover with the potato. Bake at 180°C/ Gas mark 4 for about 20 minutes or until it begins to brown.

STEAK AND GUINNESS

600g braising steak, cubed; Flour; A knob of butter;
200g mushrooms, sliced; 2 large onions, sliced;
2 large carrots, sliced; 330ml Guinness;
300ml hot chicken stock; A bay leaf; 3 sprigs of thyme;
1 tsp tomato purée; 1 tbsp Worcestershire sauce;
300g puff pastry; 1 egg, beaten

1 Dust the beef in flour. Heat oil in a pan and cook the beef in batches until browned, about 5 minutes. Remove the beef and add butter. Cook the mushrooms, onions and carrots until soft, 5 minutes. Add Guinness and reduce by half. Return the beef with the stock, bay, thyme, purée and Worcestershire. Simmer for 1½ hours. Transfer to a pie dish.

2 Roll the pastry out on a floured surface. Dampen the dish edges and cover with pastry. Crimp the edges, cut off the excess and brush with egg. Cook at 190°C/Gas mark 5 for 30–40 minutes or until golden.

CHICKEN AND MUSHROOM

4 chicken breasts, diced; 150g button mushrooms, sliced;
1 onion, diced; 1 garlic clove, chopped; 50g butter;
1 tbsp flour; 200ml stock; 300ml milk; 10g tarragon;
350g shortcrust pastry; 1 egg, beaten

1 Heat oil in a pan. Cook the chicken, mushrooms, onion and garlic for 5–8 minutes until coloured. Take off the heat. Melt the butter in a saucepan, add the flour and stir for 2 minutes. Gradually add the stock, beating to prevent lumps. Add the milk and simmer gently for 10 minutes, stirring constantly or until the sauce has thickened. Stir in the tarragon, season well and mix with the chicken mixture. Spoon into a pie dish.

2 Roll the pastry out on a floured surface. Dampen the dish, lay over the pastry, crimp the edge and egg wash. Cook at 180°C/ Gas mark 4 for 20–25 minutes until golden.

FISH PIE

1kg potatoes; 150g butter; 2 leeks, finely chopped;
2 tsp English mustard; 600ml double cream;
Juice of 1 lemon; A handful of parsley, chopped;
600g smoked haddock fillets; 40g cheddar, grated

1 Put the potatoes on to boil. Meanwhile, melt 50g butter in a pan and cook the leeks gently with a lid on until soft. Remove from the heat. Add the mustard, cream, lemon juice and parsley. Season well. Cut the haddock into bite-sized pieces and arrange in a pie dish. Pour over the leek sauce.

2 Once the potatoes are cooked and easily pierced with a knife, mash them with the remaining butter. Spread the potato over the fish and sprinkle over the grated cheese. Cook at 180°C/Gas mark 4 for 40 minutes or until golden.

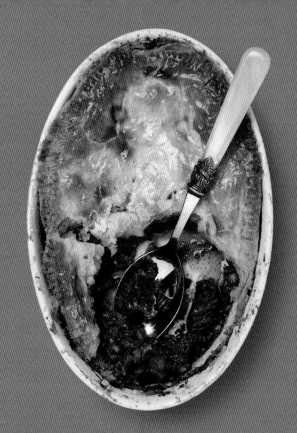
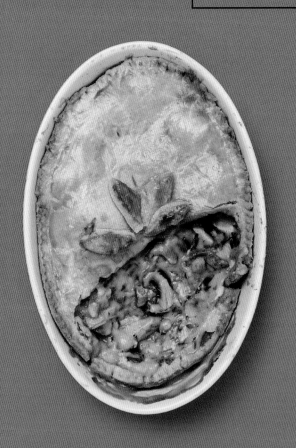

SAVOURY PIES

BEEF AND MANGETOUT

Groundnut oil; 400g rump steak, cut into thin strips;
2 garlic cloves, crushed; 2 handfuls of baby corn;
1 tbsp soy sauce; 2cm knob of ginger, grated;
2 tsp sesame oil; 1 tsp cornflour;
150ml hot chicken stock; 2 handfuls of mangetout;
2 tbsp oyster sauce

1 Heat the wok until very hot, add a little groundnut oil and stir-fry the beef for 2–3 minutes. Remove the beef from the pan, add a splash more oil and stir-fry the garlic and baby corn for 2 minutes.

2 Add the soy sauce, ginger, sesame oil, cornflour and hot stock. Cook for 2 minutes, then add the mangetout and cook for another minute.

3 Return the beef to the pan and add the oyster sauce. Warm through for 2–3 minutes. Add some seasoning and serve.

CHICKEN AND GARLIC

6 garlic cloves, crushed; 5cm knob of ginger, chopped;
3–4 spring onions, chopped;
3–4 chicken breasts, cut into strips;
200ml chicken stock; 1 tbsp caster sugar;
2 tbsp soy sauce; 2 tsp cornflour; 375g sugar snap peas;
A pinch of chilli flakes; 1 red pepper, chopped;
Cooked rice, to serve

1 Stir-fry half the garlic with all the ginger and onions in hot oil for 2 minutes. Add the chicken and cook for 3 minutes to seal.

2 In a bowl, mix together the stock, sugar, soy sauce and cornflour until smooth. Add the mixture to the wok with the remaining garlic, the peas, chilli and pepper. Cook for 6–8 minutes or until the sauce has thickened and the chicken is cooked. Serve with rice.

PAD THAI

350g rice noodles; 2 red chillies, chopped;
2 garlic cloves, crushed; 5cm knob of ginger, chopped;
6 spring onions, chopped; 2 eggs, beaten;
2 tbsp fine sugar; Juice of 2 limes; 4 tbsp fish sauce;
2 tbsp soy sauce; 100g peanuts;
300g cooked prawns; 2 handfuls of beansprouts;
A handful of coriander, chopped

1 Soak the noodles in hot water until soft. Drain. In a wok, stir-fry the chillies, garlic, ginger and onions in oil over a high heat for 5 minutes or until the onions are soft.

2 Add the eggs and cook for 1 minute until scrambled. Add the sugar, lime juice, fish sauce, soy sauce and noodles. Toss together for 1 minute. Add the peanuts, prawns and beansprouts. Cook for 2 minutes, sprinkle with the coriander and serve.

SWEET AND SOUR

450g chicken or pork, diced;
5cm knob of ginger, chopped;
4 garlic cloves, crushed; 500g mixed stir-fry vegetables;
227g tin of pineapple chunks, drained; 1 tbsp fine sugar;
2 tbsp rice vinegar; 3 tbsp rice wine or dry sherry;
2 tbsp soy sauce; 150ml chicken stock;
1 tbsp cornflour, mixed with a little water to form a paste;
2 tbsp tomato purée; Cooked rice, to serve

1 Using a wok, stir-fry the chicken or pork with the ginger and garlic in hot oil for 2–3 minutes or until sealed. Add the stir-fry vegetables and cook for 2–3 minutes.

2 Stir in all of the remaining ingredients. Simmer for 5 minutes or until the meat is cooked through. Serve with some rice.

CHICKEN IN BBQ SAUCE

1 onion, chopped; 3 garlic cloves, crushed;
5cm knob of ginger, grated; A pinch of chilli flakes;
3 tbsp vinegar; 1 tbsp Worcestershire sauce;
2 tsp smoked paprika; 400g tin of chopped tomatoes;
2 tbsp tomato ketchup; 3 tbsp soft brown sugar;
8 chicken thighs and drumsticks, deboned and skin on

1 Fry the onion, garlic, ginger and chilli gently in olive oil for about 10 minutes or until softened. Season. Add the vinegar, cook for 1 minute then add Worcestershire sauce, paprika, tomatoes, ketchup and sugar. Cook gently for about 1 hour, uncovered, until the sauce has thickened. Leave to cool.

2 Marinate the chicken thighs in the cold sauce for between 4 and 12 hours. Grill on a medium heat barbecue or under the grill for about 10 minutes, turning and brushing with more of the marinade regularly.

BARBECUE

SARDINES WITH CHERMOULA

A handful of coriander
2 garlic cloves
2 tsp paprika
1 tsp cumin seeds
1 red chilli
A pinch of saffron strands
4 tbsp olive oil
Juice of 1 lemon
12 sardines or small mackerel, gutted and heads removed

1 Place all the ingredients except the fish into a blender and pulse to combine to a smooth paste. Season with some salt.

2 Marinate the fish for 30 minutes. Grill on a hot barbecue or under the grill for 3–5 minutes on each side, brushing with more marinade as they cook.

LAMB WITH MINT HOLLANDAISE

500g leg of lamb, deboned; 4 tbsp white wine vinegar;
3–4 peppercorns; 1 shallot, sliced; 2 sprigs of mint;
3 egg yolks; 175g butter, diced; A squeeze of lemon juice

1 Season the lamb and cook over a medium heat barbecue for about 30 minutes, turning every 5 minutes or so. Once cooked, cover in tin foil and allow to rest.

2 Boil the vinegar with the peppercorns, shallot and 1 sprig of mint until reduced by half. Strain into a heavy-based pan. Add the yolks and whisk constantly over a low heat (you should be able to touch the sides of the pan) until the egg thickens. Gradually add the butter, whisking to incorporate.

3 Pour into a dish. Add the lemon juice and seasoning and stir in the torn leaves of the remaining mint. Serve with the lamb.

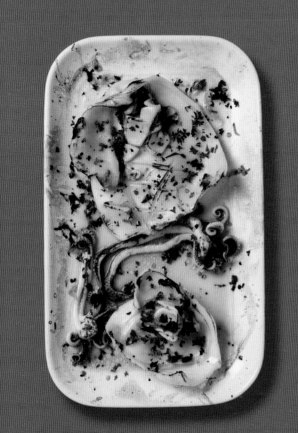

SQUID

4 squid, well cleaned and guts discarded
Juice and zest of 1 lemon, extra for serving
3 tbsp olive oil
A pinch of chilli flakes
A small handful of parsley, chopped

1 Cut down one side of the squid's body tubes to open and make crosshatched scores on the outside of each using a sharp knife. Mix together the lemon juice and zest, olive oil and chilli flakes, and add the squid. Leave to marinate for 1 hour.

2 Cook on a hot barbecue or under the grill for 90 seconds on each side. Serve with the parsley scattered over the top and some more lemon juice squeezed over.

DESSERTS

AND DRINKS

BERRY FOOL

450g mixed berries
2–3 tbsp caster sugar
225ml whipping cream, extra for serving

1 Place the berries and sugar in a pan with a few tbsp of water. Bring to the boil and cook for about 5 minutes or until the fruit has softened.

2 Purée in a blender and sieve out the pips. In a bowl, beat the cream until softly whipped and combine with the smooth berry mixture. Serve with an extra swirl of unwhipped cream.

BERRY MESS

225ml double cream
2 tbsp icing sugar
4 meringues, broken into pieces
300g mixed berries

1 In a bowl, whip the cream until it forms soft peaks.

2 Gently fold in the icing sugar. Crumble over the meringues and berries and serve.

BERRY AND YOGHURT SMOOTHIE

400g mixed berries, plus extra for serving
6 heaped tbsp low-fat natural yoghurt
300ml milk
3–4 tbsp icing sugar or maple syrup

1 Place all the ingredients in a blender and whiz until smooth, sweetening the mixture to taste.

2 Decorate with some extra berries and serve chilled.

FROZEN BERRIES WITH WHITE CHOCOLATE

300ml double cream
2 sprigs of mint, extra for serving
200g white chocolate, broken into pieces
500g frozen mixed berries

1 Heat the cream and mint in a small pan until just boiling. Turn off the heat and leave to infuse for 30 minutes. Once infused, remove the mint.

2 Place the cream back over a low heat and add the chocolate. Gently warm through, stirring constantly, until the chocolate has melted and the mixture is glossy – about 5 minutes. Place the frozen berries in a serving dish and pour over the melted chocolate mixture. Decorate with some extra mint leaves and serve.

BERRIES

APPLE

350g sweet shortcrust pastry; Plain flour, for dusting;
5–6 cooking apples; A knob of butter; 1 cinnamon stick;
1 tsp vanilla extract; 3 tbsp icing sugar

1 Roll out the pastry on a floured surface until about 25x25cm. Line a 20cm flan tin. Push into the corners and cut away any excess. Chill for 30 minutes.

2 Core, peel and chop 3 of the apples. Cook with the butter, cinnamon, vanilla and 1 tbsp of sugar in a covered pan until soft, about 20 minutes. Discard the cinnamon, purée until smooth and leave to cool. Pour into the pastry base. Core and finely slice the rest of the apples and arrange on top of the purée. Sprinkle over the remaining sugar.

3 Cook the tart at 180°C/Gas mark 4 for 30–40 minutes or until the apples are caramelised and the pastry is golden.

SWEET TARTS

LEMON

350g sweet shortcrust pastry; Plain flour, for dusting;
5 eggs, beaten; 150ml double cream; 150g caster sugar;
3 lemons; 1 tbsp icing sugar

1 Roll out the pastry on a floured surface until about 25x25cm. Line a 20cm flan tin. Gently push the pastry into the corners and cut away any excess. Chill for 30 minutes. Cover with greaseproof paper and weigh down with baking beans. Bake at 180°C/Gas mark 4 for 15 minutes. Remove the beans and paper and cook for a further 10–15 minutes or until the base is golden.

2 Combine the eggs, cream and sugar with the zest of 2 lemons and the juice of all 3. Pour into the pastry case. Cook for a further 30 minutes or until the lemon mixture is set but still wobbly. Dust with icing sugar. Serve.

FRUIT

300g all-butter puff pastry; Icing sugar, for dusting; 150ml double cream; 150g custard; 1 tsp vanilla extract; 400g mixed summer berries

1 Roll out the pastry on a surface dusted with icing sugar until about 25x25cm. Line a 20cm flan tin. Gently push the pastry into the corners and cut away any excess. Chill for 30 minutes. Cover with greaseproof paper and weigh down with baking beans. Bake at 180°C/Gas mark 4 for 15 minutes. Remove the beans and paper and cook for a further 10–15 minutes or until the base is golden. Leave to cool.

2 Whip the cream until thick. Combine with the custard and vanilla. Chill for 30 minutes to thicken.

3 Just before serving, pour the mixture into the case. Cover with the fruit and serve.

TREACLE

350g sweet shortcrust pastry
Plain flour, for dusting
5 tbsp golden syrup
5 handfuls of fresh breadcrumbs
Juice and zest of 1 lemon

1 Roll out the pastry on a floured surface until about 25x25cm. Line a 20cm flan tin. Push into the corners and cut away any excess. Chill for 30 minutes.

2 Warm the golden syrup in a pan until runny. Add the breadcrumbs and lemon, stir well and pour into the chilled tart case.

3 Cook at 180°C/Gas mark 4 for 40 minutes or until the top begins to brown and the pastry is golden.

BANANA AND CHOCOLATE

4 large ripe bananas, peeled
75g icing sugar
Juice of 1 lemon
150ml double cream
150ml Greek yoghurt
50g dark chocolate, finely grated

1 Place the bananas, sugar and lemon juice into a blender. Purée until smooth.

2 Whip the cream to form soft peaks. Fold in the yoghurt and the fruit purée. Chill for 30 minutes.

3 Sprinkle over the chocolate and serve.

LEMON AND RASPBERRY

200ml double cream
200ml Greek yoghurt
300g lemon curd
A handful of basil leaves, finely chopped
A handful of raspberries, slightly squashed

1 Whip the cream to form soft peaks. Fold in the yoghurt, lemon curd and basil. Chill for 30 minutes.

2 Top with the crushed raspberries. Serve.

MANGO FOOL

3 ripe mangoes
3 tbsp icing sugar
200ml double cream
200ml Greek yoghurt
1 tsp vanilla extract
2 sprigs of mint, chopped

1 Peel and stone the mangoes. Place 2 of the mangoes in a blender with 1 tbsp of icing sugar. Purée and sieve.

2 Whip the cream to form soft peaks. Fold in the yoghurt, vanilla, remaining sugar and the fruit purée. Chill for 30 minutes.

3 Slice the third mango and place on top of the fool. Sprinkle with mint and serve.

RHUBARB FOOL

500g rhubarb, cut into batons
A small knob of butter
75g caster sugar
2cm knob of ginger, grated
200ml double cream
200ml Greek yoghurt
2 tbsp icing sugar

1 Place the rhubarb in a saucepan with the butter, sugar and ginger. Cover the pan and leave to cook gently for about 10 minutes or until soft. Allow to cool.

2 Whip the cream to form soft peaks. Fold in the yoghurt, icing sugar and the rhubarb with all its liquid. Chill for 30 minutes. Serve.

FOOLS

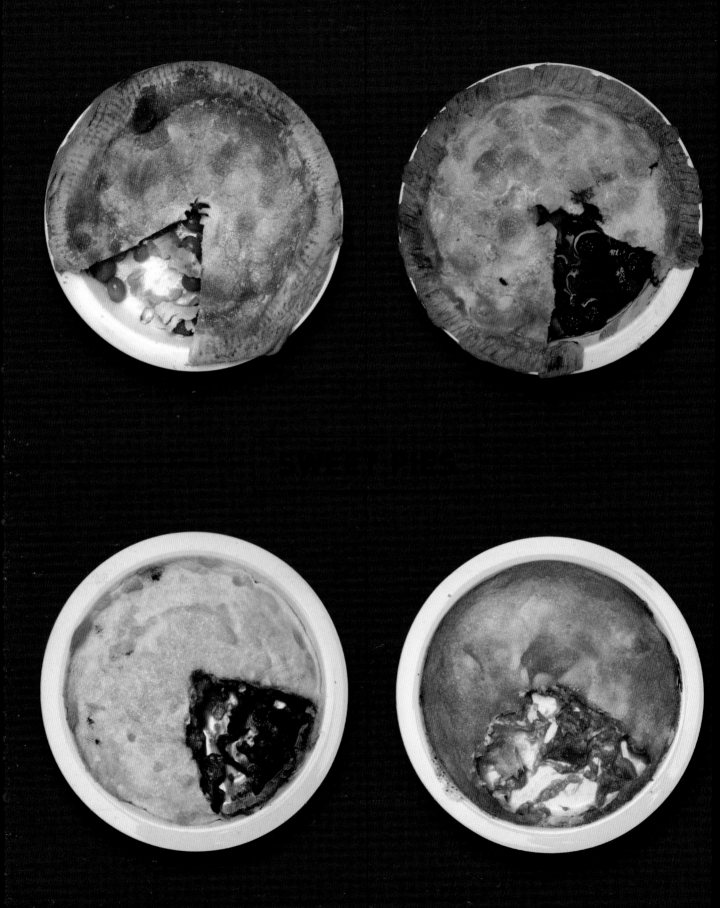

GOOSEBERRY

600g gooseberries
4 tbsp caster sugar
300g sweet shortcrust pastry
Plain flour, for dusting
1 egg, beaten

1 Top and tail the gooseberries. Place in a shallow pie dish and sprinkle with 3 tbsp of the sugar.

2 Roll out the pastry on a floured surface until large enough to cover the pie dish. Wet the edges of the pie dish and place the pastry over the top. Press down and crimp the edges with a fork and cut off any excess. Brush the top with the egg. Sprinkle over the remaining sugar. Cut a hole in the centre to allow steam to escape. Cook for 40 minutes at 190°C/Gas mark 5 until golden.

BLACKBERRY AND APPLE

4 small cooking apples; 250g blackberries;
3 tbsp caster sugar; 300g sweet shortcrust pastry;
Flour, for dusting; 1 egg, beaten

1 Peel and core the apples and cut into small chunks. Place in a shallow pie dish with all of the blackberries. Sprinkle with 2 tbsp of the sugar.

2 Roll out the pastry on a floured surface until large enough to cover the pie dish. Wet the edges of the pie dish and place the pastry over the top. Press down and crimp the edges with a fork and cut off any excess. Brush the top with the egg. Sprinkle over the remaining sugar. Cut a hole in the centre to allow steam to escape. Cook for 40 minutes at 190°C/Gas mark 5 until golden.

PLUM

12 plums; Juice and zest of 1 orange;
4 tbsp caster sugar; A large knob of butter;
3 tbsp ground almonds; 3 eggs, separated

1 Quarter and stone the plums. Place the plums in a saucepan with the orange juice and zest, 2 tbsp of the sugar and the butter. Cover and cook gently until collapsed, about 10–15 minutes. Transfer to a shallow pie dish and leave to cool slightly. Stir in the ground almonds and the egg yolks.

2 Whisk the egg whites until stiff. Add 1 tbsp of sugar and whisk until glossy. Spread over the plums and sprinkle with the remaining sugar. Cook for 20 minutes at 180°C/Gas mark 4 or until golden.

RHUBARB

500g rhubarb; 5 tbsp caster sugar;
Juice and zest of 1 orange; A large knob of butter;
4 tbsp ground almonds; 3 eggs, separated

1 Cut the rhubarb into chunks. Place in a saucepan with 3 tbsp of the sugar, the orange juice and zest and the butter. Cover and cook gently until collapsed, about 10–15 minutes. Transfer to shallow pie dish and leave to cool slightly. Stir in the ground almonds and the egg yolks.

2 Whisk the egg whites until stiff. Add 1 tbsp sugar and whisk until glossy. Spread over the rhubarb and sprinkle with the remaining sugar. Cook for 20 minutes at 180°C/Gas mark 4 or until golden.

CHOCOLATE

125g butter, at room temperature; 75g caster sugar;
1 tsp vanilla extract; 80g chocolate, finely grated;
125g plain flour

1 Beat together the butter, sugar and vanilla until pale and fluffy. Add the chocolate and sift in the flour. Mix to form a soft dough.

2 Place the dough on some greaseproof paper and roll into an even log shape. Wrap and chill for 1 hour.

3 Cut the log into 2cm rounds. Place the rounds onto 2 greased baking sheets, making sure that there is plenty of space between each and cook for 15–20 minutes at 170°C/Gas mark 3 until they are golden but still soft in middle. Cool on a wire rack. Serve.

118

SWEET BISCUITS

NUT

125g butter, at room temperature
75g caster sugar
1 tsp vanilla extract
A handful of mixed nuts, chopped
125g plain flour

1 Beat together the butter, sugar and vanilla until pale and fluffy. Add the nuts and sift in the flour. Combine to form a soft dough.

2 Place the dough on some greaseproof paper and roll into an even log shape. Wrap and chill for 1 hour.

3 Cut the log into 2cm rounds. Place the rounds onto 2 greased baking sheets, making sure that there is plenty of space between each and cook for 15–20 minutes at 170°C/Gas mark 3 until they are golden but still soft in middle. Cool on a wire rack. Serve.

LEMON

125g butter, at room temperature
75g caster sugar
1 tsp vanilla extract
Zest of 2 lemons
125g plain flour

1 Beat together the butter, sugar and vanilla until pale and fluffy. Add the lemon zest and sift in the flour. Mix to form a soft dough.

2 Place the dough on some greaseproof paper and roll into an even log shape. Wrap and chill for 1 hour.

3 Cut the log into 2cm rounds. Place the rounds onto 2 greased baking sheets, making sure that there is plenty of space between each and cook for 15–20 minutes at 170°C/Gas mark 3 until they are golden but still soft in middle. Cool on a wire rack. Serve.

ORANGE AND CARDAMOM

125g butter, at room temperature; 75g caster sugar;
1 tsp vanilla extract; 5 cardamom pods;
125g plain flour; Zest of 1 orange

1 Beat together the butter, sugar and vanilla until pale and fluffy.

2 Pierce the cardamoms with a knife, extract the seeds and discard the shell. Crush the seeds in a pestle and mortar. Add to the butter mixture, along with the sifted flour and orange zest. Mix to form a soft dough. Place on greaseproof paper and roll into a log shape. Wrap and chill for 1 hour.

3 Cut the log into 2cm rounds. Place, spaced out, onto 2 greased baking sheets and cook for 15–20 minutes at 170°C/Gas mark 3 until they are golden but still soft in middle. Cool on a wire rack. Serve.

CLASSIC

100g pudding rice; 410g tin of evaporated milk; 600ml milk; 30g caster sugar; 1 tsp vanilla extract; 1 tsp grated nutmeg; Jam, to serve

1 Place the rice, evaporated milk, milk, sugar and vanilla in an ovenproof casserole dish. Slowly bring to a gentle simmer on the hob and leave to cook, stirring occasionally, for about 10 minutes or until the rice begins to soften.

2 Sprinkle over the nutmeg. Transfer the dish to a 150°C/Gas mark 2 oven, uncovered if you like skin, covered if you do not. Cook for 1 hour or until it reaches the creamy consistency that you want. Serve with a dollop of your favourite jam.

EMPRESS

100g pudding rice; 410g tin of evaporated milk; 600ml milk; 30g caster sugar; Zest of 1 lemon, extra for serving; 1 tsp vanilla extract; 4 tbsp custard

1 Place the rice, evaporated milk, milk, sugar, lemon zest and vanilla in an ovenproof casserole dish. Slowly bring to a gentle simmer on the hob and leave to cook, stirring occasionally, for about 10 minutes or until the rice begins to soften.

2 Transfer the dish to a 150°C/Gas mark 2 oven, uncovered if you like skin, covered if you do not. Cook for 1 hour or until it reaches the creamy consistency that you want. Leave to cool. Stir in the custard, sprinkle with some gratings of lemon zest and serve cold.

COCONUT

100g pudding rice; 400g tin of coconut milk; 600ml milk; 50g caster sugar; 1 tsp vanilla extract; 3 tbsp desiccated coconut; 425g tin of mango slices, drained

1 Place the rice, coconut milk, milk, sugar and vanilla in an ovenproof casserole dish. Slowly bring to a gentle simmer on the hob and leave to cook, stirring occasionally, for about 10 minutes or until the rice begins to soften.

2 Transfer the dish to a 150°C/Gas mark 2 oven, uncovered if you like skin, covered if you do not. Cook for 1 hour or until it reaches a creamy consistency. Toast the coconut under the grill. Top the rice pudding with some mango slices and toasted coconut and serve.

SPICED

8 cardamom pods; 100g pudding rice; 410g tin of evaporated milk; 600ml milk; 30g caster sugar; 1 cinnamon stick; 1 tsp vanilla extract; 1 tsp grated nutmeg; A handful of almonds, chopped

1 Pierce the cardamom pods with a knife. Extract the seeds, discard the shells and crush in a pestle and mortar. Place the seeds, rice, evaporated milk, milk, sugar, cinnamon, vanilla and nutmeg in an ovenproof casserole dish. Bring to a gentle simmer on the hob and leave, stirring occasionally, for about 10 minutes or until the rice begins to soften.

2 Transfer the dish to a 150°C/Gas mark 2 oven, uncovered if you like skin, covered if you do not. Cook for 1 hour or until it reaches a creamy consistency. Serve either warm or cold, sprinkled with the nuts.

RICE PUDDING

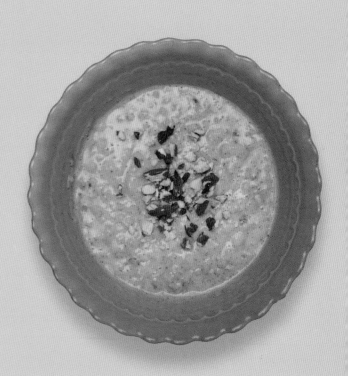

STRAWBERRIES

BALSAMIC VINEGAR

400g strawberries
4 tbsp balsamic vinegar
4 tbsp caster sugar
Vanilla ice cream, to serve

1 Hull and quarter the strawberries. Drizzle with the vinegar and sprinkle over the sugar. Leave for 1–2 hours to marinate. Serve with a spoonful of vanilla ice cream.

BASIL AND STAR ANISE

200ml water
100g caster sugar
A large handful of basil, extra for serving
2 star anise
400g strawberries
Crème fraîche, to serve

1 Bring the water and sugar to the boil in a saucepan with the basil and the star anise. Simmer for 5 minutes to form a syrup. Leave to cool.

2 Hull and quarter the strawberries. Strain the syrup, discarding the basil and star anise. Pour the syrup over the strawberries. Serve with a dollop of crème fraîche and a few basil leaves.

VANILLA SUGAR

4 tbsp caster sugar
½ vanilla pod
400g strawberries
Crème fraîche, to serve

1 Place the sugar and vanilla pod in a spice grinder, or small food processor. Blitz until a very fine paste. Place in a jar and leave to absorb the flavour as long as possible (this can be weeks or months).

2 Hull and quarter the strawberries. Sprinkle with the sugar and leave in a warm place for 1 hour to marinate. Serve with a dollop of crème fraîche.

ELDERFLOWER AND PROSECCO

100g caster sugar
100ml water
Zest and juice of 1 lemon
75ml elderflower cordial
400g strawberries
300ml chilled prosecco

1 Boil the sugar, water and lemon zest in a small saucepan for 5 minutes or until the consistency of syrup. Leave to cool. Stir in the cordial and lemon juice.

2 Hull and quarter the strawberries. Drizzle over the syrup. Top with the prosecco just before serving.

BANANA

200g plain flour; 1 tsp baking powder; 275ml milk;
1 egg; 2 ripe bananas, extra for serving;
1 tbsp caster sugar; 50g butter, melted;
Crème fraîche and maple syrup, to serve

1 Whisk together the flour, baking powder, milk and egg in a large mixing bowl until combined. Mash the bananas and add to the batter along with the sugar and butter. Stir until well mixed.

2 Heat an oiled frying pan. Once hot, add a large spoonful of the batter and cook for about 30 seconds on each side or until the pancake begins to bubble and brown. Serve with some sliced bananas, crème fraîche and a drizzle of maple syrup.

SWEET PANCAKES

COCONUT AND PINEAPPLE

200g plain flour; 2 tsp baking powder; 275ml milk;
1 egg; 2 tbsp caster sugar; 50g butter, melted;
A large handful of desiccated coconut;
1 small pineapple, peeled and cut into chunks;
3 tbsp icing sugar

1 Whisk together the flour, baking powder, milk and egg in a large mixing bowl until combined. Add the sugar, butter and desiccated coconut to the batter and stir until well mixed.

2 Heat an oiled frying pan. Once hot, add a large spoonful of the batter and cook for about 30 seconds on each side, or until the pancake begins to bubble and brown.

3 Dust the pineapple with the icing sugar and sear in a hot dry pan until lightly caramelised. Serve on top of the pancakes.

ORANGE

200g plain flour; 1 tsp baking powder; 275ml milk;
1 egg; 100g butter; 2 tbsp caster sugar; 2 oranges;
3 tbsp Grand Marnier or Cointreau

1 Whisk together the flour, baking powder, milk and egg in a bowl until combined. Melt 50g of the butter and stir into the batter.

2 Heat an oiled frying pan. Once hot, add a large spoonful of the batter and cook for about 30 seconds on each side or until it begins to bubble and brown. Keep warm.

3 Heat the sugar in a hot dry pan, without stirring, until it melts and turns a caramel colour. Take off the heat and whisk in the remaining butter. Stir in the juice of the 2 oranges. Ignore any lumps. Place back on the heat. Add the liqueur and the zest of 1 orange and gently cook until reduced and sticky. Pour over the pancakes and serve.

BLUEBERRY

200g plain flour; 1 tsp baking powder;
275ml milk; 1 egg; 2 tbsp caster sugar;
50g butter, melted;
200g blueberries, extra for serving;
Icing sugar, to serve

1 Whisk together the flour, baking powder, milk and egg in a large mixing bowl until combined. Add the sugar, butter and whole blueberries to the batter and stir until mixed.

2 Heat an oiled frying pan. Once hot, add a large spoonful of the batter and cook for about 30 seconds on each side or until the pancake begins to bubble and brown. Serve topped with some extra blueberries and a dusting of icing sugar.

APPLE AND CHOCOLATE

4 cooking apples
75g Demerara sugar
2 Mars bars or other caramel chocolate bars
100g butter
150g plain flour

1 Core and peel the apples and cut into rough chunks. Place in a baking dish and sprinkle with a tbsp of the sugar. Cut the chocolate bars into chunks and add to the dish of apples.

2 Place the butter and flour in a food processor and pulse until the mixture resembles coarse breadcrumbs. Stir in the remaining sugar.

3 Sprinkle the crumble mixture over the apples and bake at 180°C/Gas mark 4 for 40 minutes or until golden.

MIXED BERRY AND BANANA

500g frozen mixed berries
4 bananas, sliced
100g butter
100g plain flour
50g Demerara sugar
75g rolled oats

1 Place the frozen berries and banana slices in a baking dish.

2 Place the butter and flour in a food processor and pulse until the mixture resembles coarse breadcrumbs. Stir in the sugar and the oats.

3 Sprinkle the crumble mixture over the berries and bananas. Bake at 180°C/Gas mark 4 for 40 minutes or until golden.

PLUM AND ALMOND

12 plums; 75g granulated sugar;
1 tsp ground cinnamon; 75g butter;
100g plain flour; 50g ground almonds
A handful of flaked almonds

1 Cut the plums in half, remove the stones and place in a baking dish. Sprinkle with 1 tbsp of the sugar and the cinnamon.

2 Place the butter and flour in a food processor and pulse until the mixture resembles coarse breadcrumbs. Stir in the ground and the flaked almonds and the remaining sugar.

3 Sprinkle the crumble mixture over the plums and cook at 180°C/Gas mark 4 for about 40 minutes or until golden.

RHUBARB AND GINGER

600g rhubarb
Juice and zest of 1 orange
50g caster sugar
6 ginger nuts
100g plain flour
50g butter
4 tsp ground ginger

1 Cut the rhubarb into 5cm lengths. Place in a baking dish with the orange juice, zest and the sugar. Bake at 180°C/Gas mark 4 for 10 minutes or until slightly golden.

2 Place all of the remaining ingredients in a food processor and pulse until the mixture is the texture of coarse breadcrumbs. Scatter the crumble mixture over the rhubarb. Return to the oven and bake for a further 40 minutes or until golden.

CRUMBLES

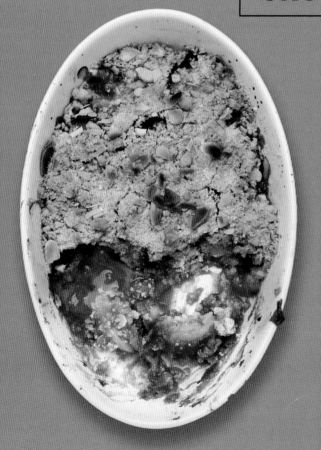
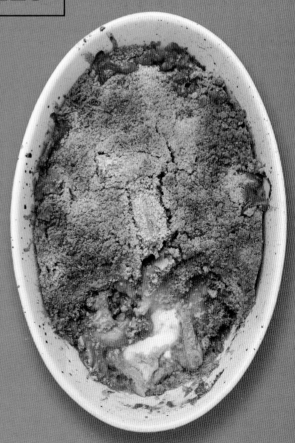

CHOCOLATE

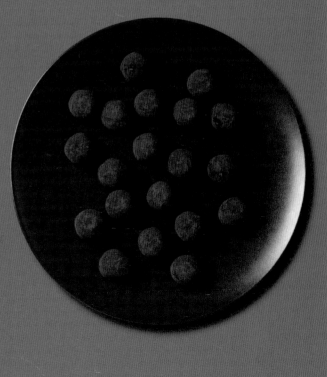

BROWNIES

200g butter; 200g dark chocolate; 4 eggs;
300g Demerara sugar; 1 tsp vanilla extract;
150g plain flour; 2 handfuls of walnuts, chopped

1 Place the butter and chocolate in a heatproof bowl and melt over a saucepan of boiling water (the base should not touch the water) or in a microwave on high for about 1½ minutes. Stir. Leave to cool.

2 Beat together the eggs, sugar and vanilla until thickened, about 5 minutes. Add the chocolate mixture and stir to combine. Sift in the flour and fold in gently, along with nuts.

3 Pour into a 23cm square cake tin lined with baking paper. Bake at 180°C/Gas mark 4 for 25 minutes or until firm on top but slightly squidgy in the middle. Remove from the tin and place on a wire rack. Leave to cool. Cut into 12 or 16 squares and serve.

HAZELNUT SPREAD

100g hazelnuts; 75g dark chocolate;
75g milk chocolate; 30g butter;
2 tbsp hazelnut oil; Slices of toast, to serve

1 Roast the nuts at 180°C/Gas mark 4 for 10 minutes. Place in the middle of a clean tea towel and rub to remove the skins of the nuts. Roughly chop.

2 Place the chocolates and butter in a heatproof bowl and melt over a saucepan of boiling water (the base should not touch the water) or in a microwave on high for 1½ minutes. Stir. Leave to cool.

3 Blend the melted chocolate with 75g of the nuts until as fine as possible. Pass through a sieve and place in a jar.

4 Stir in the remaining nuts and the oil. Serve on slices of toast.

MOUSSE

150g milk chocolate
3 tbsp double cream
3 eggs, separated
A handful of mixed nuts, chopped

1 Place the chocolate and the cream in a heatproof bowl and melt over a saucepan of boiling water (the base should not touch the water) or in a microwave on high for 1½ minutes. Add the egg yolks and beat together. Leave to cool.

2 Whisk the egg whites to form soft peaks. Gradually fold the egg whites into the chocolate mixture. Spoon into serving bowls and chill for at least 2 hours. Sprinkle with the nuts just before serving.

TRUFFLES

150ml double cream
Cardamom pods, chilli, cinnamon or mint (optional)
200g dark chocolate, grated
3 tbsp cocoa powder, chopped nuts or desiccated coconut

1 Bring the cream to the boil in a small saucepan. Add one of the flavourings if you like, allow to infuse for 20 minutes, strain and then bring the cream back to the boil.

2 Pour the hot cream over the chocolate and whisk until smooth. Chill for 1 hour.

3 Dust your hands with some cocoa powder and scoop out a ball of the chocolate using a teaspoon. Use the palms of your hands to roll the mixture into even-sized balls. Roll these through more cocoa powder, nuts or desiccated coconut to decorate and chill.

CHOCOLATE

1 Toast a slice of brioche. Top with a small handful of grated dark chocolate. Drizzle with a little olive oil and a sprinkling of sea salt.

BANANA AND ALMOND

1 Toast a slice of brioche. Top with a mashed banana, a handful of flaked almonds and 1 tsp of ground cinnamon. Place under the grill for 1 minute or until the almonds are lightly toasted.

MASCARPONE AND STRAWBERRY

1 Toast a slice of brioche. Spread with 2 tbsp of mascarpone and 2 hulled and sliced strawberries. Drizzle with 1 tsp of honey.

FIG AND GOAT'S CHEESE

1 Toast a slice of brioche. Top with 2 tbsp of goat's cheese, 1 sliced fig and a few walnut halves. Drizzle with 1 tsp of honey and heat under the grill for 1 minute before serving.

SWEET TOASTS

SESAME AND MAPLE SYRUP

1 Toast a slice of brioche. Spread with 1 tsp of tahini paste and drizzle over 3–4 tsp of maple syrup.

CHOCOLATE AND PEAR

1 Toast a slice of brioche. Spread with 1 tbsp of chocolate spread or the hazelnut spread shown on page 131. Top with a large slice of pear.

DOLCELATTE AND APPLE

1 Toast a slice of brioche. Spread with *Torta di Dolcelatte* (this is Dolcelatte layered with mascarpone) and top with a sliced apple and a few chopped sage leaves.

CHERRIES AND ALMONDS

1 Toast a slice of brioche. Top with a handful of jarred cherries (ideally in Kirsch) and drizzle over some of the syrup that they sit in. Scatter with a handful of flaked almonds, dust with a little icing sugar and place under the grill for 1 minute to caramelise.

SWEET
TOASTS

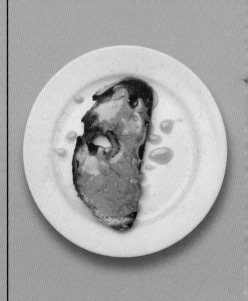

CHEDDAR AND CARAWAY

75g butter, cubed
75g plain flour
75g cheddar, grated
2 tsp caraway seeds

1 Place all of the ingredients in a food processor. Blitz to form a dough. Roll into an even log shape, wrap in clingfilm and chill for 30 minutes.

2 Cut into 1cm rounds, place, spaced apart, on a greased baking sheet and cook at 180°C/Gas mark 4 for about 15 minutes or until golden.

CHEESE BISCUITS

PARMESAN AND FENNEL

75g butter, cubed
75g plain flour
75g Parmesan, freshly grated
1 tsp mustard powder
2 tsp fennel seeds

1 Place all of the ingredients in a food processor. Blitz to form a dough. Roll into an even log shape, wrap in clingfilm and chill for 30 minutes.

2 Cut into 1cm rounds, place, spaced apart, on a greased baking sheet and cook at 180°C/Gas mark 4 for about 15 minutes or until golden.

PARMESAN AND CHILLI

75g butter, cubed
75g plain flour
75g Parmesan, freshly grated
1 tsp chilli flakes

1 Place all of the ingredients in a food processor. Blitz to form a dough. Roll into an even log shape, wrap in clingfilm and chill for 30 minutes.

2 Cut into 1cm rounds, place, spaced apart, on a greased baking sheet and cook at 180°C/Gas mark 4 for about 15 minutes or until golden.

STILTON AND WALNUT

75g butter, cubed
75g plain flour
75g Stilton, crumbled
A handful of walnuts, chopped

1 Place all of the ingredients in a food processor. Blitz to form a dough. Roll into an even log shape, wrap in clingfilm and chill for 30 minutes.

2 Cut into 1cm rounds, place, spaced apart, on a greased baking sheet and cook at 180°C/Gas mark 4 for about 15 minutes or until golden.

CORDIALS

ELDERFLOWER

1 Bring 250g sugar, 400ml water and the pared zest of 1 lemon and 1 orange to the boil. Simmer for 10 minutes to form a syrup. Clean 10 elderflower heads, removing bugs and leaves. Add to the syrup with the juice of 1 lemon and 1 orange. Leave to infuse overnight. Strain. Keep in the fridge. Serve diluted to taste.

SUMMER BERRY

1 Bring 8 tbsp caster sugar, 1kg frozen mixed berries and the pared zest of 1 lemon to the boil. Simmer for 10 minutes to form a syrup. Strain, pushing the berries with the back of a ladle to extract the juice. Add the juice of 1 lemon. Keep in the fridge. Serve diluted to taste.

LEMONGRASS AND GINGER

1 Slice 3 lemongrass stalks and hit with a rolling pin to bruise. Put in a pan with a 1in piece of grated ginger and the pared zest of 2 lemons. Add 250g sugar and 400ml water. Bring to the boil. Simmer for 10 minutes to form a syrup. Add the juice of 2 lemons and leave to cool. Strain. Keep in the fridge. Serve diluted.

ORANGE

1 Bring 100g caster sugar, 150ml water, pared zest of 1 lemon and pared zest of 6 oranges to the boil and simmer for 10 minutes to form a syrup. Add the juice of the 6 oranges and 1 lemon and check for sweetness. Strain and leave to cool. Keep in the fridge. Serve diluted to taste.

LEMON AND MINT

1 Bring 200g caster sugar, 300ml water, a large handful of mint, the pared zest of 2 lemons as well as the juice of 10 lemons to the boil. Simmer for 10 minutes to form a syrup. Remove from the heat and leave to completely cool. Strain. Keep in the fridge. Serve diluted to taste.

POMEGRANATE

1 Bring 3 tbsp caster sugar and the juice and seeds of 5 pomegranates to the boil. Simmer for 10 minutes to form a syrup. Add the juice of 2 lemons and leave to cool. Strain. Keep in the fridge. Serve diluted to taste.

PASSION FRUIT

1 Heat 100g sugar and 150ml water until the sugar has melted. Add the pulp of 20 passion fruit and the juice of 1 lemon. Simmer for 10 minutes to form a syrup. Leave to cool. Strain, pushing the pulp with the back of a ladle to only leave behind the pips. Keep in the fridge. Serve diluted to taste.

RASPBERRY AND VANILLA

1 Bring 500g raspberries, 4 tbsp caster sugar, pared zest of 1 lemon and 2 split vanilla pods to the boil with 100ml water. Simmer for 10 minutes to form a syrup. Strain – squash the berries leaving only the pips behind. Add the juice of 1 lemon. Refrigerate. Shake before serving. Dilute to taste.

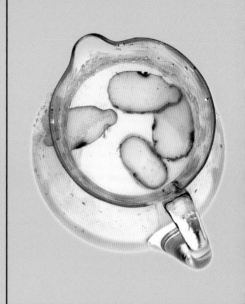

CORDIALS

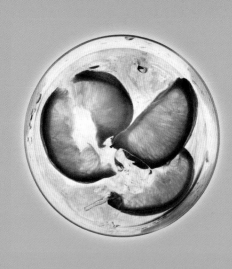
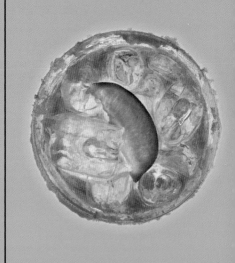

CLASSIC COCKTAILS

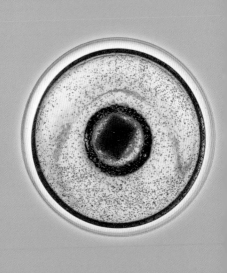
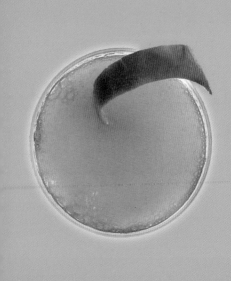

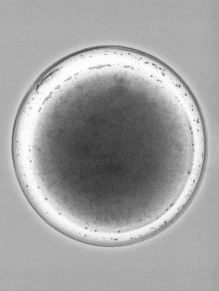

NEGRONI

1 Chill a tumbler glass, then fill with ice. In a shaker filled with ice, shake together 30ml gin, 30ml Campari and 30ml sweet vermouth. Strain into the chilled glass. Serve garnished with a twist of orange.

MOJITO

1 Strip the leaves from 1 sprig of mint and place in a tall glass. Squeeze in the juice of 1 lime and add 2 tsp fine sugar. Crush the sugar and mint with a pestle and mortar. Add 60ml white rum and top up with soda water. Garnish with lime wedges and serve immediately.

MARGARITA

1 Squeeze the juice of half a lime around the edge of a tall glass. Dip into a bowl of crushed sea salt. Fill with ice. In a shaker filled with ice, shake together 30ml tequila gold with 15ml Cointreau. Strain into the glass. Garnish with a lime wedge and serve.

BLOODY MARY

1 Place ice in a tall glass. Add 60ml vodka, 125ml tomato juice, a few drops of Tabasco and Worcestershire sauce, a dash of dry sherry and a squeeze of lemon juice and stir. Garnish with a pinch of celery salt, some pepper and a stick of celery. Serve.

CLASSIC COCKTAILS

CHAMPAGNE

1 Place a sugar cube in a champagne flute. Add 2 dashes of angostura bitters and 30ml brandy. Top up with some champagne or sparkling wine and serve immediately.

MIMOSA

1 Chill a champagne flute. Half fill with champagne. Top up with 60ml of orange juice and 15ml of Triple Sec. Garnish with a twist of orange peel and serve immediately.

KIR ROYALE

1 Pour 1 tsp of cremé de cassis into a champagne flute. Top up with some champagne and serve immediately.

BELLINI

1 Blitz half a white peach in a food processor with a dash of water and some icing sugar if it is not very juicy. Pour the peach purée into a champagne flute. Top up with champagne and serve immediately.

DIRTY MARTINI

1 Chill a martini glass. In a shaker half filled with ice, stir together 60ml gin or vodka, 15ml dry vermouth and a dash of olive brine. Stir for 30 seconds. Strain into the chilled glass. Garnish with an olive skewered on a cocktail stick and serve immediately.

DAIQUIRI

1 Chill a martini glass. Gently bring 2 parts water and 1 part sugar to the boil, stirring occasionally, until the sugar has dissolved and become a syrup. In a shaker half filled with ice, shake together 60ml white rum, juice of half a lime and a dash of sugar syrup for 30 seconds. Strain into the glass. Garnish with a wedge of lime and serve.

PINA COLADA

1 Chill a tall glass. Place 30ml dark rum, 30ml Malibu, 60ml coconut cream, 60ml pineapple juice and a few ice cubes into a blender and blitz until smooth. Pour into the glass and garnish with a piece of pineapple and a cherry skewered on a cocktail stick and serve immediately.

DRY MARTINI

1 Chill a martini glass. In a shaker half filled with ice, stir together 60ml gin or vodka and 15ml dry vermouth for 30 seconds. Strain into the glass. Garnish with a twist of lemon peel. Serve immediately.

PARTY COCKTAILS

SEX ON THE BEACH

1 Chill a tall glass. In a shaker half filled with ice, shake together 60ml vodka, 30ml peach schnapps, 15ml cremé de cassis, 60ml orange juice and 60ml cranberry juice. Strain into the glass. Garnish with a slice of orange and serve.

PINEAPPLE MARTINI

1 Chill a martini glass. Gently bring 2 parts water and 1 part sugar to the boil, stirring occasionally, until it has become a syrup. Crush a piece of pineapple with 30ml syrup in the bottom of a cocktail shaker. Add ice, 60ml vodka and 30ml lemon juice. Stir together. Strain into the glass and garnish with a piece of pineapple.

MAI TAI

1 Half fill a tall glass with ice. In a shaker half filled with ice, shake together 60ml white rum, 30ml Triple Sec, juice of 1 lime, 60ml pineapple juice, 60ml orange juice and 2 mint leaves. Shake for 30 seconds. Strain into the glass. Garnish with some mint and pineapple and lime wedges skewered on a cocktail stick. Serve.

ROOSEVELT MARTINI

1 Chill a martini glass. In a shaker half filled with ice, stir together 60ml gin and 15ml vermouth. Stir for 30 seconds. Strain into the glass. Garnish with 2 different olives skewered on a cocktail stick. Serve immediately.

ACKNOWLEDGEMENTS

I'd like to start by thanking Nicola Jeal, Saturday Editor at *The Times*, for giving me the chance to try out the initial recipe column on an unsuspecting readership and for reining me in when I tried to get too clever. Her mantra of 'quicker, easier' was, of course, spot on. Thanks also to the hugely talented Romas Foord, whose clean images and handy way with a rolling pin set the tone for the column and now the book. Special praise for the subeditors on the *Saturday Times Magazine*, led by the fantastic Amanda Linfoot, who have saved me from many an embarrassing slip-up over the years. I owe you all.

Thank you to all the chefs I've had the privilege to interview and watch at work over the years – Gordon Ramsay, Mark Sargeant, Marcus Wareing, Theo Randall, Jason Atherton, Angela Hartnett, Eric Chavot, Pierre Koffmann, Anthony Demetre... too many to mention. You've been so generous with your time and I've learnt so much from all of you.

I'm very grateful to my agent, Karolina Sutton at Curtis Brown, for being so unerringly enthusiastic and supportive about the project and, of course, to Anne Furniss and Alison Cathie at Quadrille for taking me on. Thanks also to the whole team – Helen, Louise, Gemma and Nicola, for making the book look so good and read so well and to Ed for putting it out there.

Finally special thanks to my wonderful wife, Amanda, whose constant support and encouragement have got me where I am today, and to my three beautiful children, Oliver, Isabella and Georgia-Rose, who helped so assiduously with the eating (4 ways with chocolate. Yippee!).